WHAT I'VE LEARNED

Motivation, Inspiration and Strategy for the Professional Martial Artist

By Rob Colasanti

Published by NAPMA, LLC
5601 116th Avenue North
Clearwater, FL 33760
1-800-973-6734

Printed and Bound in USA

Editor: Herb Borkland
Design and typesetting: Bryan R. Hudson
Cover photography: Bill Bly
Accounting: William Colasanti
Printing: Paragon Press

ISBN 0-9755254-0-9

Table of Contents

Acknowledgements

As I wrote the Acknowledgements portion of this book, I realized how many incredible people have helped shape me into the person that I am today. I'm truly grateful, and I have so many wonderful people to thank.

For starters, I'd like to recognize a few of my colleagues within the martial arts industry, whose knowledge and wisdom have had a profound impact on my development. My deepest appreciation goes out to Rick Bell, Bill and Milan Bly, the Cokinos family, John Corcoran, Joe Corley, Larry Doke, Charlie Foxman, Jeff Frick, Joe Galea, Jim Graden, Tommy Lee, Stephen Oliver, Jeff Smith, Steve Stewart, and Bob Wall. It's an honor to have learned something special from each of you.

Next, I wish to thank all of my martial arts friends and heroes who have inspired me to the bone, and supported me along the way. An extended, heartfelt bow goes out to Fred and Katie Degerberg, Fumio Demura, Stephen Hayes, Willie "The Bam" Johnson, Bill Kipp, Cung Le, Joe Lewis, Kathy Long, Tom Patire, Peyton Quinn, Dan "The Beast" Severn, Frank Shamrock, Ernie Reyes, Sr., Grand Master Jhoon Rhee, Mike Swain, Keith Vitali, and Don "The Dragon" Wilson.

Also, I can't put into words how much I will always appreciate the steady guidance and golden opportunities that were given to me by NAPMA's founder, and my first martial arts instructor, Mr. John Graden. Thank you, sir, for everything!

My hat goes off to NAPMA's Executive Team and the NSSN Faculty Members for all that they do. I've never met a more dedicated and creative bunch of professionals. NAPMA remains the world's largest professional martial arts association, and continues to change lives, for a reason. It's because of you!

I'd like to thank our cherished NAPMA members, all over the world. We value your support more than you could ever imagine. Without you, NAPMA and this book would never have been possible.

In addition, I want to thank my good friend Dr. Frederick S. Freed for treating my martial arts related injuries for almost twenty years now. Thanks, Doc, for always being there. A double high-five goes out to Adrienne Johnson of Coca-Cola Enterprises. If she did not believe in my vision, I would never have been able to create the NAPMA/Coca-Cola program for the martial arts industry.

Finally, I want to thank my loving family: my grandparents William and Rita, my father Bob, and my uncle William. I can never repay you for all the support you've given me throughout the years.

Last, but certainly not least, I want to thank my beautiful fiancé, Anja Lee, for all that she is, and all that she does. You're the best of the best. I love you!

Foreword

I've seen the martial arts industry evolve tremendously since I first brought Taekwondo to America in 1956. Collectively, we've journeyed a long way and I'm so very proud of the progress our industry has made in such a short period of time.

In fact, today's schools are more professional and profitable than ever before in the history of the martial arts. Why? A major reason is because school owners now have a huge advantage over their predecessors. They have access to extremely affordable, top quality information products and services. These valuable resources have literally transformed our industry by giving instructors all the tools they need to succeed and prosper in the martial arts business world.

Over the past decade, one individual who has been at the very forefront of the movement towards professionalism is Rob Colasanti. A third-degree black belt in my lineage, I have known Rob for many years. I can tell you that he lives by the martial arts philosophy - "The Lead By Example Action Philosophy." I'm proud to say that I have seen him consistently apply the universal basic value, truth, to his steadfast mission of helping the martial arts industry to grow.

Since 1995, Rob Colasanti has had his finger on the pulse of the martial arts industry. His hard work and dedication has lead him to become a respected leader among leaders in our field. Yet, Rob has never lost his humility or his focus. He stays on track just like a true martial artist should. Always learning, always growing, always giving back.

Rob has played a major role in making martial arts business information mainstream. This indelible contribution has helped countless instructors to take their schools to the next level. In this book, Rob will share with you what he has learned as President of the world's largest professional martial arts association - NAPMA. I encourage you to put this valuable information to good use so that through the martial arts we can all continue to change the lives of our students one kick at a time and ultimately make our country a better place for all.

With My Love,

Jhoongoo Rhee

Grand Master Jhoon Rhee

Introduction

It was October of 1994. I was a young third-degree black belt, and a professional martial artist with nine years experience under my belt. Besides martial arts, the other focus in my life was going to medical school.

At the time, I had just completed 191 credit hours of college, graduated USF with a biology degree, and even survived the grueling Medical College Aptitude Test (MCAT). Even though the martial arts were coursing through my veins, I was spending more time in a lab coat than I was in a gi. I had to. I was in the final stages before heading off to become Dr. Colasanti, and I was fully prepared to meet the challenge head on.

Then, as I rolled into 1995, I was met with some pretty disappointing news. My MCAT scores were not competitive enough to be accepted into USF's Medical School, which I had my heart set on. I knew that this was going to delay my journey by at least one semester, and I was extremely bummed out. I felt like I had lost a championship fight that I spent years training for. But I stayed positive, and quickly registered to take the exam again later on that year.

In the meantime, I was kind of in limbo. Since I had given up my nine-year employment at USA Karate in St. Petersburg, Florida in order to focus full-time on my education, I had no job and very little money.

It was around this time when John Graden mentioned to me that he had just launched an organization called the National Association of Professional Martial Artists, and offered me the opportunity to work for him out of his house one day a week. All I had to do was make follow-up calls every Wednesday night for a few hours, and ask school owners to join. I was to be paid a commission for each member I enrolled, and I gladly accepted the offer. I figured it would help me get by for a few months before I left for medical school.

So it was then that I began my NAPMA career in a spare bedroom with an old Macintosh 520c laptop computer, a phone, and a list of contacts. Pretty much blind as to what I was selling, I picked up the phone, and began trying to enroll school owners in this thing called NAPMA.

A New Career is Born

As NAPMA's first official employee, I began producing big results FAST—and I was quickly given the title of Membership Director. As a veteran Program Director at USA Karate, I had been selling martial arts memberships for many years. Selling NAPMA memberships was very similar, but even easier.

With all the new memberships I was generating, my hours were immediately increased. Soon I was working full-time for NAPMA, and I actually put medical school on hold. I'd teach private lessons in the morning at USA Karate, and then head right over to my office in the spare bedroom. Often, I was still sweating, and sometimes still bleeding from that morning's sparring session. But after a quick shower and a change of clothes, I'd start burning up the phone lines. I hit it hard all day, everyday, including weekends, for more than a year. I was building our membership base, and I was building it in a hurry. This was the same thing I used to do at the martial arts school, only this time I was engaged in a higher purpose—helping the martial arts industry to grow!

At the time, selling NAPMA memberships was a piece of cake. The reasons for this are now obvious to me. First of all, martial arts business information was not nearly as accessible or affordable then, as it is today. NAPMA made it very easy for schools to become involved by removing all of the common barriers to entry, such as style, cost, ranking, etc. Second, I had valuable knowledge of the martial arts school business. Interestingly enough, I realized right away that even though I was young, even though I was only a lowly third degree consulting with "masters," in most cases I knew a whole lot more about how to run a school than they did. This was key. Third, I had very strong diagnostic selling skills. One truly needs this when selling memberships. (We'll discuss this later on.) All combined, this skill-set, along with proper timing, made it quite simple for me to generate members and keep them coming back for more.

Before long I had enrolled five hundred NAPMA members, then six hundred, then we totally outgrew the spare bedroom and moved into our first building. In fact, I had enrolled over 1,000 members into NAPMA before we even had a second employee in the membership department. Soon we began hiring additional staff members, the Martial Arts Professional magazine was born, we were conducting seminars all over the US, and in 1997 I became the company's very proud Vice President. We were blazing new trails, and everyday at NAPMA was like climbing aboard a runaway train. That's when I truly began to learn most of the knowledge I'm going to share with you in this book…

NAPMA…My Laboratory

As NAPMA continued to evolve, I continued to absorb knowledge like a sponge. For many years, I spent most of my days on the phone with martial arts school owners. I literally spoke to thousands of them, representing every style, background, and affiliation imaginable. In fact, during this time I don't know of anyone in the martial arts field that was speaking to more school owners on a regular basis than myself. I heard it all, constantly, from all corners of the industry. Daily, I was exposed to the challenges, successes, complaints, statistics, ideas, requests, and unique situations of instructors throughout North America.

NAPMA had become my laboratory, and it gave me a crash course on the martial arts school business that expanded my knowledge light years beyond what I had learned at USA Karate. Because of my hard work, integrity, dedication, and ability to consistently produce strong results, I was able to earn the respect of many of the martial arts industry's top decision-makers in a relatively short period of time. I felt like I was on the fast track to success. Then, in January of 2003, I was once again promoted. I had become the President of NAPMA.

We Built Something Amazing

I'm proud to say that NAPMA's extremely hardworking and creative team built the largest professional martial arts association in the world. At our peak, the NAPMA organization reached approximately 2,100 active members representing more than twenty countries around the world. We certified over 6,000 instructors through our nationwide Cardio Karate seminar tour, during the big Fitness Kickboxing boom in the late nineties. Our popular World Conference became the largest professional martial arts convention and trade show that the industry had ever seen. And, our magazine, the Martial Arts Professional, was reaching over 25,000 schools and instructors per month.

In retrospect, I believe it was the NAPMA organization that took the movement towards professionalism in our industry to a whole new level. We had the courage to subordinate our wallets to our values, blaze new trails, and speak out against many of the restrictive traditions that were holding instructors back. But most importantly, we made martial arts information products mainstream, and as a result we changed the lives of countless instructors and, subsequently, their students. What an amazing ride, what an amazing accomplishment... that's NAPMA's legacy!

What This Book Will Do for You

That leads me to why I've decided to write this book. During my nineteen year journey as a professional martial artist, and now as the President of NAPMA, I've learned scores about what it takes to be highly successful in the incredible field we've chosen. In addition, I've had the unique opportunity to work closely with many of the sharpest business minds, celebrity instructors, and top school owners our industry has ever known. So what does this mean for you?

This is your big chance to siphon volumes of valuable information out of my brain, and put it into yours. To learn my best tips, tactics, advice, and trade secrets. By reading this book, you will learn from my mistakes as well as my successes. You will garner motivation, inspiration, and practical, proven knowledge that will help you take your personal and professional goals to the next level and beyond.

Sir or ma'am, my goal with this book is to give you the tools you need to transform your school into a safer, better, and more value-oriented place for your students, and to help you increase your profits, in the process. Ready to sharpen your edge? Then start reading. Put this incredible information to good use, and make the commitment right now to never stop growing as a professional martial artist.

Here now is my gift to you. This is **What I've Learned...**

1: An Evolution of Professionalism

At NAPMA, we're able to forecast changes in the industry long before most. Our radar never shuts down, and we constantly observe the entire field from a "bell-tower-like" position. With that thought in mind, I wanted to alert you as to an industry-shaping phenomenon that's currently taking place.

Right now, the martial arts industry is transforming, consolidating, metamorphosing. In the process, a high percentage of schools are going out of business. Typically, they are small, understaffed, low-budget, anti-education, part-time schools that only offer one service. These types of schools are fast joining the ranks of the dinosaurs. At the same time the larger, more professional, multi-service schools seem to be flourishing in increasing amounts. It appears as if our industry is growing, yet shrinking at the same time. It's consolidating.

While certain types of schools are shutting down, others are reaching new heights. In fact, we're seeing more schools with larger student counts, generating higher incomes than ever before in the history of the martial arts. The number of schools grossing over a million dollars a year is constantly climbing. We're talking about martial arts here, folks.

The reality is that big numbers are not uncommon anymore. It's because, as an industry, we're finally starting to get our act together. We're like the Ugly Duckling in transition. The telltale signs pointing to an evolution of professionalism are beaming bright, and I'm not the only one who has noticed them.

Recently I had the pleasure of eating lunch with a top executive from Nike. A twenty-year veteran of the famous footwear-company, he's seen many industries transform from being antiquated, fragmented, and uneducated to modern, unified, and professional. From the outside looking in, his perception was that the martial arts industry was transforming this way too. In his words, "Martial arts is starting to become a truly professional industry." What a great compliment to hear from a Nike bigwig!

By comparison, what's occurring in martial arts right now is similar to what took place in sporting goods, home improvement, footwear, auto parts, restaurants, and many other industries. It's true. Many of the small, lackadaisical, mom-and-pop shops in these fields disappeared, and consumers now do the majority of their shopping at supercenters like Home Depot, Sports Authority, Discount Auto Parts, and Wal-Mart, as examples.

Now that's certainly not meant to imply that you have to "sell-out", become huge, or develop a multi-school operation in order to survive. In all fields, small, top-quality specialists have always done well for themselves. They've carved out a niche amongst the competition, and even charge a premium for their services. However, the key is that they provide a top-quality service and a fantastic overall experience.

As our industry becomes more and more professional, my advice to you is to make sure your school does the same. It's best to ride the horse in the direction it's going, or else your school will eventually become the exception. The evolution towards professionalism will force all of us to all work a little bit harder. I'm proud to say that NAPMA continues to fuel this movement. The bar is raising. In the end, it's the best thing for our students.

2: The 1-2-3 Punch Combination That Always Scores A Knock Out

It's interesting to talk to black belts across the country, and find out just how, or why, they got into the martial arts school business. I often inquire as to what made them select teaching as their profession of choice. As you'll read below, they report a number of different reasons. Here are a few of the more common cases.

Case #1 - PASSION
Most often, a black belt becomes a school owner because he has a true passion for the arts. Owning a school will allow him to remain in his comfort zone, and continue doing what he loves to do most: teaching martial arts.

Case #2 - ORPHANAGE
Other black belts open schools because they become orphaned. This occurs, for example, when they relocate, or leave their school on bad terms. Also, black belts can become orphans if their instructor's school goes out of business. Regardless of the circumstances, the point is that they get disconnected from their instructor somewhere along the way, and go on to open their own school.

Case #3 - INHERITANCE
Sometimes a black belt will become an owner when the school's main instructor retires, or expires. In order to prevent the school's tradition from dying, a senior student will typically take the helm. Usually, this black belt is the highest-ranking student in the school, and feels obligated to "carry the torch."

Case #4 - EXPANSION
A black belt can become an owner when the school's main instructor expands into multiple locations, or starts a franchise.

Case #5 - INCOME
Opening a school enables black belts to earn a living. They realize that not only will they be able to train full-time, but, better yet, they'll get paid for it, too. Martial arts simply becomes their trade.

Case #6 - TRANSFER
Many black belts build a following of students by teaching out of a variety of locations such as local community centers, YMCA's, health clubs, churches, etc. An effective strategy, they transfer all the students from these separate locations into one centrally located school.

Clearly, our industry is comprised of a diverse bunch of professionals who opened schools for a variety of different reasons. Regardless of how you ended up in the business, you have one thing in common with everybody else. Now that you own a martial arts school, which is also a business, it's your responsibility to make it successful!

School owners... here's a simple 1-2-3 punch combination that will help you reach your goals and achieve peak performance in the very unique business that you've chosen.

1. Create A Vision (The Jab): Many great fighters have claimed that the jab is the most important punch. It allows one to bridge-the-gap, and to set up other, more powerful techniques. As a school owner, having a clear-cut vision as to where you'd eventually like to take your school, is just as important as having a good jab. It is, indeed, the critical first step towards success.

Furthermore, your vision will help you to create a defined set of goals. Write these goals down, and review them regularly. They will add meaning to your actions, and give you direction. Just remember that all great achievements begin with a vision and a specific set of goals. What are yours?

2. Seek Education (The Reverse Punch): Think of education as being the reverse punch in our 1-2-3 punch combination. In other words, once you have a vision as to where you'd like to take your school, you'll then need continuous education to provide you with the tools to make it happen.

There are numerous companies out there, like NAPMA, that specialize in helping martial arts schools strengthen their business. Their support is very affordable, and it can thrust your school light-years into the future. You simply have to be willing to try new ideas, and make use of the plentiful information that exists all around you.

3. Follow-Through on Your Ideas (The Hook): You've stunned the opponent with your jab, and staggered him with your reverse punch. Now, it's time to knock him out with the hook! In business, this means following-through on the many ideas that education provides. It's just as important as coming back with the hook when sparring.

Once education teaches you what to do, then you simply have to do it! Take action on your ideas, and finish what you've started. You've got to complete the job in order to be successful. Otherwise, your education becomes wasted knowledge, and your vision can't happen. Without a doubt, follow-through is the "punch" that really makes the difference when trying to make your vision come true.

In conclusion, it doesn't matter how you ended up owning a school. The point is that you do. Now, it's your responsibility to make the most of it. So remember to use your 1-2-3 punch combination as you fight your way to the top, and turn your vision into a reality.

Section Two

3: There's Never Been a Better Time to Become "Successful"

I've learned that in the martial arts business, success is a relative term. That's why I never tell instructors to become more successful until I first understand what "success" means to them. Let me explain.

Some instructors I speak with associate success with earning a lot of money or having a lot of students. In their eyes, bigger is better. They want to make a million bucks, and they're not going to be satisfied until the day comes when they can proudly gawk at seven digits in their bank account.

However, other instructors I know do not see money or legions of students as success. They're more interested in quality of life. They want less stress, less responsibilities, and more free time. To them, success is going fishing on the weekends, having more time to spend with their family, or just being able to spar in the middle of the week if they feel like it. As I said, everyone has a different definition of success.

So I'm not going to cram my definition of success down your throat. You have to define it for yourself based upon your values and the vision you have for your future. However, I will tell you that there has never been a better time in the history of the martial arts for you to become "successful" once you determine what success means to you.

Without a doubt, martial arts business information is now more readily available than ever before. These days, you can easily and inexpensively get your hands on the success secrets of a smorgasbord of top owners with proven track records. Information on preschool curriculums, after-school martial arts, retention strategies, fitness courses, Internet services, entire business systems, and a zillion other how-to programs and alternate profit centers are right under your nose. Plus, most of today's information providers give you higher quality information and more of it for a fraction of what it used to cost.

For these reasons and others, I'm of the opinion that there are no more excuses for having a lack of "success" in the martial arts business. There are just too many resources out there that can show you the way. At the same time, however, success is a matter of choice. No great idea works by itself. You still have to put in the required effort if you want to see results. That takes self-discipline and hard work. It's kind of like earning a black belt and you're no stranger to that.

So how can this information evolution benefit you? For starters, the beauty of today's information products is that they allow you to trim years off your learning curve. They save you precious time. Plus, they can help you increase quality, profitability, retention, and overall professionalism. Why try to reinvent the wheel if you don't have to? It's a whole lot easier to learn from the past mistakes and successes of others that have already been where you want to go. It's a no-brainer.

On this note, my advice to you is simple. First, define "success." Make sure you have a crystal clear definition of what that word means to you and how it translates to the vision you have for your school. Second, start investing in a quality information service like NAPMA that can help you reach your goals quicker and more efficiently. Third, implement what you learn and always stay focused on being your absolute best. Take these three steps, and you'll put your school on the fast track to success. I've seen countless others do it, and you can, too.

In a very short period of time, the martial arts industry has evolved out of the Stone Age and into the Information Age. I see this as a tremendous opportunity for all instructors regardless of style, background, or affiliation. I believe that information is power, and it's all around us in great abundance. I strongly encourage you to take full advantage of it.

4: Don't "Dim Mok" Yourself

Throughout the centuries, there has always been a certain mystique surrounding the martial arts - Chi power, the killer-blow theory, the dance of death. At some point, I think we were all fascinated by mysteries such as these.

To me, one of the most interesting of all such tales is the dim mok. Legend has it that certain Chinese kung-fu experts possessed the ability to kill an opponent days, weeks, or even months after delivering this fatal technique. Known also as the "delayed death touch", the grave aftereffects of the dim mok would silently come calling long after the fight was over. The end result...death!

While there is no proof that the dim mok actually exists in the world of fighting, it definitely exists in other areas of our lives. Analogously, "the delayed death touch" strikes most often when it comes to poor decision-making skills. In other words, the decisions we make today usually effect us days, weeks, months, or even years later. So to ensure a successful future, we must start making quality decisions now.

Having good decision-making skills is especially important if you own or operate a martial arts school. Realize that if you fall into this category, then you are a manager. And, as a manager you will spend a lot of your time making decisions. Therefore, having excellent decision-making skills is vital to your success.

Here are three very simple tips that will help you improve your ability to make great executive decisions every time. Indeed, these are the best ways to block a dim mok.

1. Think It Through

The first step in becoming an excellent decision-maker is to gather as much information about your decisions as possible. Research is key. In order to make sensible decisions you must first have factual information to work with. Know the potential pros and cons your decision may create so you can establish a risk tolerance. Also, remember to always "think" before you "do" and avoid rushing into important decisions. This is a strategy that will help reduce your chances of being hit with a dim mok later on when the results of your decision come to fruition.

2. Learn to Fight Procrastination

When it comes to decision-making skills, a common area of weakness among managers is procrastination. That's because having to make certain decisions can be stressful, painful, and even emotionally challenging at times. So the tendency is to delay big decisions for as long as possible. Often, this results in a self-inflicted dim mok.

As Anthony Robbins says, "Human beings inherently seek pleasure and avoid pain." But to be the most effective decision-maker possible, you have to condition yourself to do the opposite. Blitz forward and attack difficult decisions, immediately. Don't put them off. The longer you wait, the more you increase your chances for incurring a missed opportunity, or creating a crisis.

3. Don't Be Too Autocratic
In the martial arts field, many owners/managers are too autocratic when it comes to making decisions. In my opinion, this is because school owners are used to being in control all of the time. Mix this with a high-flying ego, and a belt that outranks everyone else's, and you end up with an autocratic decision-maker.

When you're too autocratic you risk missing the big-picture. You develop tunnel vision, or a very narrow-minded viewpoint of the overall situation. That's why studies indicate that the best managers are democratic decision-makers. They seek the opinions of their staff, other managers, and the individuals that will be most effected by the decision at hand. They listen carefully to the feedback they get, and then make an educated decision using a consensus approach.

As a school owner, there are many other dim mok decisions that you want to watch out for. They include using tradition as an excuse to avoid innovation, lack of continuing education, allowing yourself to be taken advantage by a pseudo-master, refusing to update an archaic curriculum, and not keeping good statistics. Another bigee is unwillingness to use modern ideas such as stripe exams, Black Belt Club, Fitness Kickboxing, and NAPMA membership. The effects of bad decisions such as these are not immediate. But often, you end up paying the price later.

It's true that the quality of your decisions will determine the quality of your life. In fact, the cumulative effect of all your previous decisions has caused you to end up where you are today. So whether you're happy with your current situation or not, realize that it's no accident that you are where you are. For that reason, decisions can be considered the building blocks of life. So stack your blocks high. But in the meantime, be careful not to dim mok yourself!

5: The Dirty Dozen

Each day at NAPMA, I speak with school owners that have student counts ranging from ten to over a thousand. Some of these instructors can barely make rent, while others can barely make enough room for all of their students. Naturally, I make it my business to find out why this dichotomy exists. What I've learned is that in almost all cases, unsuccessful owners have fallen victim to what I like to call the "dirty dozen."

1. Poorly Designed Curriculum
Your curriculum can make or break your school. If your curriculum is outdated, boring, too extensive, or non-age appropriate, your retention will suffer, and so will your school. Successful owners constantly tweak their curriculum so it generates higher results.

2. No Program Director
Many struggling schools have one person doing the work of both a program director and a chief instructor. In my experience, this usually leads to burnout for the owner and stunted growth for the school. Having a competent program director is an absolute must for long-term growth.

3. "White Belt" Marketing
With all due respect, many school owners are white belt marketers. As a result, they end up wasting hard-earned money on weak marketing strategies that generate poor results. Or, they don't promote their school at all. Smart owners delegate this necessary evil to companies that specialize in it.

4. Not Keeping Statistics
Owners that do not keep track of their statistics have no idea what areas of their school needs improvement. They are flying blind. On the other hand, most successful owners keep meticulous track of, and learn how to analyze, their numbers. If you do not know where you've been, it's impossible to know where you are going.

5. No System for Product Sales
Aside from tuition and special events, product sales are the other main area of a school's income. If you do not have a solid system in place for product sales, you are seriously missing out on a hot pocket of potential revenue.

6. No Leadership Team Program
Having a quality staff is considered by many to be the most important element for operating a successful school. Consequently, if you have no Leadership Team, you're going to have a very hard time finding staff members. Your Leadership Team is your present bench strength and your foundation for future staff.

7. No Structured Renewal System

Have you implemented a structured renewal system, such as a Black Belt Club? This is one of the best things you can do for both your students and your school. Most successful schools have a Black Belt Club and Masters Club. Most struggling schools do not. They just wing it.

8. Fear of Delegation

Successful owners delegate. This allows them to focus their efforts on high return activities that only they can do. The fact is that unless you learn to delegate, you'll never be able to grow your school to its maximum potential.

9. No Continuing Education

Your growth as a school owner will be proportionate with your willingness to further your own education. School owners that do not attend seminars, read school support materials, network, or listen to motivational programs are doomed to mediocrity. On the other hand, top owners are lifelong students that try to learn something new every single day.

10. No Retirement Plan

You don't want to die broke, do you? You also probably do not want to be teaching fore-balance when you're sixty-five, right? Unless you start planning for your retirement now, you just might find yourself in this exact situation later on down the road.

11. Computer Illiteracy

Not knowing how to use a computer can really slow down your productivity. It will prevent you from generating critical school reports, desktop publishing, or maximizing your usage of the Internet. Most successful owners have a computer, and they know how to use it to their benefit.

12. Getting Out of Shape

Have you been teaching too much and training too little? Are the ends of your belt a bit shorter these days? Are you eating dinner at 10 p.m. after your school shuts down? Let's hope not. Getting out of shape is one of the worst things you can let happen to yourself. It will destroy your self-confidence, image, productivity, and health. The solution is to eat properly, and make time to train – period.

As a professional martial artist, you invest a lot of time into helping your students achieve a higher quality of life. While that's a noble task to focus on, you must not forget about yourself. If you want to teach more students, earn more income, and increase the quality of your own life, then beware the dirty dozen.

6: Kick the Excuses!

Over the years, I've had the opportunity to consult with thousands of martial arts professionals. Some were teaching out of their garages, and others had built empires. The point is that I've worked with instructors on both ends of the spectrum and everyone in between. During this time, I honestly believe I've heard every excuse for lack of success that exists in our field. However, the following three reign as the all-time best of the worst.

1. The "I'm Too Busy To Be Successful" Excuse

The least creative excuse for lack of success I frequently hear is the, "I'm too busy" excuse. That's right...they're too busy to be successful. Too busy to apply a new marketing strategy, attend a seminar, watch a video, read a book, or network. Ironically, I've found that the majority of school owners who make this excuse are typically the ones that are struggling the most.

Often, all the information they need in order to make a complete turn-around is right at their fingertips. Half of the time, they've even paid for it. But they just "can't find the time to even look at it" much less apply it. Sure, a lot of good all of that valuable information will do sitting on the floor in their office. Indeed, owners that make this excuse are usually busy all right. Unfortunately, they're not busy teaching intros, enrolling students, or collecting tuition. They're "busy" working on low return activities.

The fact is that we all have the same amount of hours in a day. The difference is that some of us have learned how to use those hours for maximum return while others simply waste them. Some of the busiest doctors, lawyers, businessmen, and school owners that I know find the time to accomplish all they need to do every single day. That's because they make time, rather than excuses.

2. The "I Can't Afford To Be Successful" Excuse

Recently, I heard Anthony Robbins tell an interesting story. A guy says to him, "Tony, I'd love to come to your seminar tonight. The problem is that I just can't afford it." Instead of giving the guy a free ticket, Tony replied, "That's too bad sir, because if you can't afford it then you're obviously one of the people that need to attend my seminar the most." How's that for a wake-up call? The point is that, if you genuinely want something bad enough, don't waste time conjuring up excuses as to why you don't have it. Instead, find a way to get it.

Becoming successful is not an accident. It takes a lot of hard work, especially in the area of education. But people that don't realize the importance of learning are great at finding excuses for not being able to educate themselves. The easiest excuse for people like this to make is the "I can't afford to educate myself" excuse. The truth is that you can't afford NOT to educate yourself. There is no better investment than an investment made in knowledge. Once you have it, the knowledge can help you become more successful for the remainder of your life. You'd be surprised at how powerful this concept is. One single piece of information that's learned and applied is sometimes all it takes to make your money back a thousand-fold.

3. The "My Traditional System Is Preventing Me from Being Successful" Excuse

Another common alibi for lack of success is "tradition." Here, an owner locks himself in a cage, and then expects others to feel sorry for him as he stares out at the rest of the world with jealousy. In my experience, tradition is frequently used as another excuse for laziness and business related under-performance in our field.

I can't tell you how many times I've heard a down-on-his-luck school owner whimper something like, "I'm in a traditional system so my marketing lacks flair." Or, "That's a great idea, but I run a traditional school so I can't use it." The list of self-inflicted wounds and excuses goes on and on. The fact is that there are plenty of traditional schools out there that are highly successful. They didn't become successful on accident or by making excuses. They worked hard for it. Success is a matter of choice.

As I wrote in my first book, *How to Be a Black Belt*, "Excuses have been created by the Gods of Mediocrity to enhance procrastination and inhibit progress." It's important to realize that excuses will rule any aspect of your life for as long as you allow them to. Don't let that happen to you. Instead, be strong, be a black belt, and kick the excuses.

7: Having the Best of Both Worlds

In my life, I've had a number of mentors from whom I've learned a great deal. One of these was my immunology professor, Dr. My Lynn Dao. Among other things, Dr. Dao ran the immunology lab at the University of South Florida (USF). After earning an "A" in her immunology course, she suggested that I apply for a fellowship grant to work as a researcher in her lab. The grant was being sponsored by the American Cancer Society, and even though I thought it was a long shot, I applied.

After a few weeks had passed, Dr. Dao informed me that I had been accepted. A premedical student, at the time, I was so excited that I could hardly contain myself! So right away she gave me a white lab coat, my very own key to the lab, and assigned me a project. The purpose of our research was to gain new insights into tissue regeneration by observing the effects of calorie restriction on the partially hepatectomized rat.

Anyhow, during my fellowship, I spent a lot of time working with Dr. Dao, and learned many valuable lessons. But one of the most important things she taught me was that you've got to love your job. And when you truly enjoy your work, your work becomes your play. Dr. Dao lead her life this way, and also enjoyed the many rewards that went along with being a successful educator at the university level. She seemed to have tremendous balance in her life, and I admired her greatly for that.

As martial arts professionals, the vast majority of us love our work as much as Dr. Dao loves hers. How could we not? We work great hours, show-up in a gi, and practice martial arts all day long while students bow to us, and call us sir or ma'am. We're pretty fortunate, if you ask me. However, running a martial arts studio is sometimes not all wine and roses. While many instructors are passionate about what they do, they end up earning a salary that is well beneath their expectations. Unlike Dr. Dao, this causes them to become severely unbalanced.

As the President of NAPMA, I've had in-depth conversations regarding the martial arts business with thousands of school owners. In my discussions, I've noticed a pattern that keeps repeating itself. What I've found is that there's a lack of fundamental business knowledge that plagues many of the professionals in our field. Things like staff management, financial control, selling, negotiation, marketing, time management, and effective communication skills are indeed areas of weakness. The reason for this is clear.

You see, when black belts open their own schools, they instantly become managers of a business. However, instructors aren't required to attend a special University of Martial Arts that teaches them how to operate a successful studio before they open it. And instructors don't go to Harvard business school before they host their grand openings. Unless they have an inherent knack for it, many black belts simply have no idea how to operate a business. After all, they've been enrolled in martial arts classes, not an MBA program. In fact, many owners are the first to admit that they're "flyin' blind." So they wing it, and try to do the best they can with what they have to work with. In many cases, this results in a small school, with a weak income, and a low growth potential.

I hate to say it, but I've seen far too many extremely talented instructors and great fighters alike end up in financial despair. Some have no retirement money, bad credit, and a flat student count for years. They love what they're doing, but they have little or nothing to show for it. In my opinion, the majority of their troubles are not because they are poor martial artists. It's not because their heart isn't in their work. It's because they don't know how to run a business properly. These folks need NAPMA bad!

So if basic business skills are your limiting steps, I sincerely encourage you to study them until you become a "black belt" in those areas. Invest in audiocassettes, videotapes, college courses, books, or seminars that will get you up to speed. This will allow you to establish a balance between the enjoyment you have for your work, and the level of income you earn.

As martial arts professionals, we're already lucky enough to do what we enjoy doing most. Just as Dr. Dao taught me, this is critical if you want to be happy in life. Now, wouldn't it be great if we could match that with an income that's worthy of the service we provide? Wouldn't it be great to have the best of both worlds?

8: Superior Blackbelt, Inferior Teacher

LINE UP! QUICKLY, LET'S GO! *Ah, I see Mr. Mc Callion is still in the dressing room. Oh, here he comes now. I better start without him so everyone remembers not to be late to one of my classes. Besides, it establishes discipline when I make an example out of the students on a regular basis.*

COME TO JOONBEE! It takes hard work to become a black belt in this school. That's why most of you probably won't make it. I hope you can prove me wrong! CHARIO! KYUNGYE! Have a seat on your ankles, shut your eyes, and breathe.

Oh yeah, there's Mr. Mc Callion, still standing at the foot of the deck. I've made him squirm long enough, I guess I'll bow him in now. Mr. Mc Callion, it's so nice of you to join us this evening. You're late! Get out here, and have a seat.

Okay, what am I gonna teach tonight? While I'm figuring it out, let me smack the heavy bag with a full-power spinning crescent kick. WHACK!!! *Ah ha, little Amy-Lynn the blue belt just looked.*

Eyes closed, Amy-Lynn. You're supposed to be concentrating. Learn to focus! That's the only way you're gonna get good grades in school. *Okay, what am I doing with these guys tonight? Hmm.*

Open your eyes, and get on your first two knuckles for push-ups! Make the first ten bounce-knuckles. You'll stop on my command. Readyyy, GO! *Geez, Mrs. Jones still can't do proper push-ups.* Come on Mrs. Jones, you call those push-ups? They look more like butt-dips to me. You DID say you wanted to learn self-defense, didn't you? Quit doing push-ups like a girl, and bend those arms.

It's only been a minute, and the whole class has their arms locked, and their butts in the air...ha, listen to 'em groan. Someday, they'll thank me for this. COME ON, PEOPLE. DIG DEEP! And stay on those first two knuckles, the concrete will make 'em tough. HALF WAY THERE! *I think they have an exam coming up, maybe I should make them do kata tonight.*

Okay, everybody up! I've seen enough slop. Turn around and straighten up your uniforms. To show respect, you never face me when you do that. *I know ... we'll spar tonight! I need a good workout anyway.* Okay, gang...GEAR UP! You've got ten minutes to get your gear on, warm yourselves up, and be ready to spar. Let's go! (Clap, clap.)

Tonight I'm gonna make them sit along the wall and watch while I spar them one at a time. This is the exact same way my instructors taught me. Oh, here comes Dr. Phares the plastic surgeon.

(Dr. Phares) Mr. C., I have a sore muscle in my leg. Do I still have to spar?

Definitely! You still have one good leg and two good arms left. Get your gear on, Doc. Let's go.

(Dr. Phares) Yes, sir.

Where was I? Oh, yeah... I'm gonna start with the biggest guy first, and towards the end of the round I'll knock the wind out of him. That always impresses everyone. Hey, hey, excuse me ma'am! No water, please. I don't want you cramping up on me while we're sparring. You can wait until after class for a drink...

Now that you've had a taste of my teaching style, how would you like to learn martial arts from me? Would you enroll your children in my school? Would you trust me to teach your wife self-defense? Would you want me to work for you? If you didn't answer "no" to all of these questions, then I suggest you put this book down immediately, and contact your local shrink!

The fact is that being a talented martial artist doesn't make you a good teacher. However, a self-created continuing education program can. How to properly teach ADHD kids, reducing liability in the classroom, proper hydration, how to motivate, leadership skill development, and a million other critical topics were not part of my black belt exam - unfortunately. I'll bet they weren't part of yours, either.

I, for one, desperately needed a continuing education program like NAPMA to help fill in the gaps, and I didn't even realize it. Had I had such a program when I was teaching, I honestly believe that my classes would not have been as unprofessional, egotistical, and unsafe as they were.

So don't fall into the same trap as me. Don't be a superior blackbelt and an inferior teacher. Educate yourself!

9: Master the Art of Continuing Education

I've been speaking to school operators of every style, all over the world, day in and day out for years. In the process, I've learned that there are clear-cut reasons why some schools flourish and other schools flop. Success or failure is no accident.

What's interesting is that some instructors can barely make rent, while others can barely make enough room for all of their students. While this dichotomy exists for many reasons, one of the most prominent factors has to do with education. Instructors often struggle because they have no continuing education program in place for themselves or their staff. Or, they do not fully utilize the educational resources they have. They're not growing as professionals, and this causes their schools not to grow, either.

Look at it this way. Most martial artists wouldn't climb into the ring for a bout against a formidable opponent unless they trained for it first, right? Yet, when it comes to business this same principle usually gets thrown right out the window. For example, instructors try to teach Leadership Team members how to be effective leaders when they themselves have never studied leadership. I chat with Program Directors whose job it is to sell memberships everyday, yet they haven't had a day of sales training in their life. The same scenario often applies to marketing, teaching preschoolers, working with ADHD children, managing a staff, and every facet of operating a small business. Get the idea?

Regardless of what level your school is at, your continued growth will be proportionate with your willingness to further your own education. School operators that do not attend seminars, study selling, understand marketing, tweak their curriculum, read school support materials, network, or listen to motivational programs, typically have a much harder time achieving their goals than those that actually do these things.

Here are two great ideas that will help you increase the education and bottom line at your school, immediately.

Create a Personal Development Library

It's hard for me to put into words how important it is for you to create a personal development library for you and your staff. It's a must. Simply begin investing in educational resources such as videotapes, audiocassettes, books, seminar manuals, DVD's, magazines, CD's and CD- ROM's. After you review an item enough times, and fully understand the material, teach it to your staff.

Then, add it to the library. Over the course of time, you'll build a vast library of knowledge, which can be used for maintenance education and ongoing staff training. Best of all, the materials in your library are tax deductible.

Professional Skills Training Sessions

Friday training sessions are excellent for honing professional skills. I recommend hosting them away from your school whenever possible. For example, you might take turns gathering at different staff members' houses. Of course the current week's host would provide refreshments like coffee, juice, fruits, etc. This makes it convenient for the team to review the newest NAPMA materials, study an educational video or audiocassette, practice role-playing, or for individuals to train other team members on something they learned. Afterwards, staff members can compare notes, and discuss how the information can be applied to your school. This kind of regular training will help your staff to stay sharp.

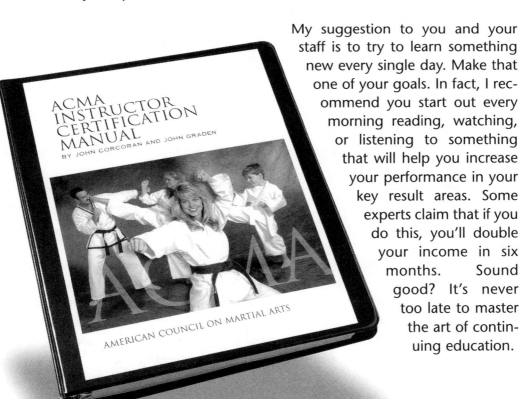

My suggestion to you and your staff is to try to learn something new every single day. Make that one of your goals. In fact, I recommend you start out every morning reading, watching, or listening to something that will help you increase your performance in your key result areas. Some experts claim that if you do this, you'll double your income in six months. Sound good? It's never too late to master the art of continuing education.

10: The Pen is Mightier Than the Sword

Would you like to dramatically improve your school's overall results? How about in key areas such as your incoming info call volume, special event registrations, image, marketing, retention, and ultimately your income? If you'd like to see quantum leaps in all of these areas and more, then my suggestion is to develop "black belt" writing skills.

Since the beginning of my career at NAPMA, writing has always been an integral part of my job. As the organization's original Membership Director, most of my writing initially included marketing letters designed to recruit members. I'd write my very best copy, and turn it in to the owner for his approval. Almost always, he'd send it back to me totally rewritten. This was frustrating, to say the least. The fact is that he was a much better writer than I was, with a lot more experience. So this pattern persisted for several years. I wrote it, he rewrote it — no matter what it was. Ahhhhhhh! But, eventually his corrections became less and less as my writing improved. Soon there were no more corrections, and I was completely autonomous in my writing for his company.

The lesson this taught me was that good writing is a skill that must be developed over time. In my experience, very few people can sit down at the keyboard, and bang out fantastic written material without any prior practice. It requires time, work, and experience - no different than earning a black belt. The key is to stay the course no matter what, because once you have solid writing skills under your belt, you massively increase your potential for personal and professional growth. At the same time, you decrease your dependency on others.

As a school owner, imagine the advantage you'll have when you can write powerful marketing pieces to prospects as easily as you throw your side kick. Think of how much better you could communicate with students and parents when you have the ability to write effective renewal letters, newsletter copy, special event speeches, bulk emails, and other written retention builders. Let's not forget the importance of being able to craft professionally written letters to politicians, community officials, local business leaders, school principals, and corporations. What about press releases, television commercials, proposals, agreements, curriculum manuals, or a book about your system? All of this is possible when you master the art of writing.

What's sad is that I've come across many topnotch martial arts professionals who have not yet figured out that the pen is mightier than the sword.

Verbally, they'll tell you all about a proven successful strategy they've been using. They'll talk your ear off about it with earth-shattering confidence. They'll sell you on it. Then, you ask them to turn it into a report, and they instantly clam-up. I've heard things like, "Uh, well, maybe I can get my mom to write it." Yet, this same person can masterfully teach the identical subject to a class full of students without giving it a moment's thought. Do you see an imbalance here?

Whether you're a white belt-wordsmith or a tenth-degree scribe-master, here are five simple tips that will help take your writing skills to the next level:

1. Practice Makes Perfect
Quality writing is a skill that must be learned and developed over time. The more you work at it the better you get. You've got to learn how to type, and practice, practice, practice.

2. Write, Read and Lead
I believe there is a direct correlation between writing, reading, and leading. Excellent leaders almost always have strong reading and writing skills. You're a leader within your school. So try to read at least one book per month. The more you read the better your writing will become, and the better leader you will be.

3. Don't Waste Good Junk Mail
Next time someone sends you an obviously well-written marketing letter or email, attempting to sell you on their product or service, don't just ditch it. Study it with the intent to improve your own business writing skills.

4. Find a Mentor
You had a martial arts mentor, right? Next, find a master writer, and become a mentee to that person. That's what I did.

5. Don't Be Too Cool for School
Signing up for a writing course can make a huge difference when it comes to learning basic sentence structure, grammatical rules, and punctuation. It may even inject some creativity into your writing style.

11: How Lack of Focus Can Kill Your School

Over the years, I've spoken to numerous school owners who nearly lost their school because they lost their focus. In most cases, the details these owners provide are the same. Based upon their descriptions, I've compiled the following story, which summarizes how lack of focus can gradually destroy a school. Don't let this happen to you!

"Mr. Jones" was a charismatic instructor who always poured his heart and soul into every class he taught. Before long, his school became successful. During the evenings, other local schools were empty while his was packed. In fact, "Mr. Jones" had at least 350 students training at his school on a regular basis. The tuition checks were rolling in, retail sales were booming, special events were huge, and his retention was nearly perfect. Plus, he had a comfortable home, a nice car, and a hearty income. After many years of hard work and dedication, he had finally made it in the martial arts business.

This is when "Mr. Jones" began to lose his focus. With visions of an early retirement, he became overconfident, and just didn't feel that it was necessary to work as hard anymore. So he put his staff in charge of the daily operations, and slowly began weaning himself away from the school more and more. Eventually, he started sleeping in on a regular basis, and taking days off in the middle of the week. In fact, golf became his new hobby.

Like many owners who lose their focus, "Mr. Jones", too, assumed his school was being run the same way that it was when he was at the helm. Unfortunately, he was wrong. In fact, his school was actually dying a slow death. Gradually, over the months, all aspects of his business were beginning to slide. But "Mr. Jones" didn't even notice the changes that were taking place…because they were occurring very slowly, and he was rarely ever there. Besides, he was busy with other things, like traveling, socializing, and exercising his vanity muscles.

As time marched on, the school became weaker and weaker. Then, one day, "Mr. Jones" finally noticed the huge decrease in his monthly EFT tuition checks. This caused him to become very concerned. So, for the first time in many months, "Mr. Jones" began spending time at the school to investigate what was going on.

What he found was not pretty. He discovered that the quality of the instruction had greatly diminished in his absence. The students were in no way inspired by the new Chief Instructor, who had only a fraction of "Mr. Jones'" experience, talent, and charisma. In fact, many of the students had switched to a local competitor's school because of this. Also, 2 4 6 calls weren't being made, outgoing sales calls had all but stopped, his enrollment conference script wasn't being followed, meetings were not being held, the Program Director was teaching his own version of an introductory lesson, etc, etc, etc! The school had taken a major nosedive.

This caused "Mr. Jones" to panic. He had a high-priced staff, a hefty rent, and a student count that looked as though it was snacked on by a school of hungry piranhas. Even more, his personal expenses were sky-high since he was used to living the lifestyle of a playboy. Suddenly, reality set in, and "Mr. Jones" realized that, because of his own neglect, his school was on the verge of going under. He was about to lose it all.

At this point, he had no choice but to demote his Chief Instructor, slash salaries to generate cash flow, and immediately take over the day to day operations of the school. "Mr. Jones" knew that he was going to have to work twice as hard to undo the mess he created. For many months, his new focus would be on trying to nurse his school back to life once again.

When consulting with the "Mr. Jones'" of the world, the above mentioned pattern of events is usually what's described. They build their school up to a comfortable level, get overconfident, lose their focus, give their staff way too much responsibility way too quickly, and then distance themselves from the school, for various reasons. At first, they think they have the perfect situation. But little by little, the piranhas set in. Eventually, there's nothing left but a pile of bones. That's when they rush back to the school in an effort to repair the damage. Sometimes, they are in time to salvage the wreck. Other times the school just dies. Either way, they end up right back on the deck doing all of the things that made their school successful in the first place.

Remember that nobody will ever care about your school as much as you do. Also, keep in mind that complacency can kill any business. So if you want to avoid becoming a "Mr. Jones", make sure you don't lose your focus.

12: Jack of All Trades, Master of One

As NAPMA's longest-standing consultant, there's a scenario that I've encountered way too many times throughout the years. A school owner calls in. Immediately, he informs me that his school is barely breaking even, and new enrollments are at an all time low. He's extremely frustrated and says he needs help before it's too late. Unless something changes, he'll have to close down. After much contemplation, I have concluded how a school owner can reach this point.

The reason is because he is a black belt trying to run a business. Aside from reading Guerrilla Marketing, who ever taught him how to operate? All these years, he's been studying martial arts, not business. Overwhelmed, the black-belt struggles to survive with a great side kick and a near perfect set of katas. But in the competitive world of business, such an arsenal does little good.

A force of one, he attempts to tackle the many tasks, besides teaching, that are critical for operating a successful commercial school. But these tasks are way outside of his area of expertise, and are usually executed with "white belt" level competence. Even so, ego stands in the way as he continues to fly-blind and wing it.

This is the common mistake that dooms many school owners to mediocrity. In fact, it has been my experience that a school will continue to suffer for as long as a black belt attempts to be a jack of all trades, when he's really only a master of one.

Consider this. Does being a black belt qualify an individual to create effective marketing strategies? Does it give someone the ability to design ad campaigns or write quality newsletters? Does it turn one into an accountant or a financial planner? How about a salesperson, counselor, computer expert, or interior decorator? Across the board the answer is NO!

The fact is that being a solid black belt alone is not nearly enough to make a school successful. That's just one important ingredient in the overall recipe for success. Unfortunately, many owners don't realize this. They're so use to being regarded as an expert in their art, that they get confused, and begin to think that they're an expert at everything. This single incorrect notion is why a lot of school owners either go out of business, or just never get their school off the ground in the first place.

I talk with so many owners that have been operating for more than a decade yet only maintain about 50-100 students. An active count such as that barely provides enough revenue to keep the lights on. Yet, others pack their schools with 200-300 students in less than a year. How? It's mainly because they've found a way to couple great martial arts instruction with an effective business plan.

It's important to realize that there are two sides to running a school. There is a teaching side and a business side. Typically, black belts are strong teachers and weak businessmen. Not always, but most of the time. Yet, most owners attempt to tackle the business side of the school even though they have very little or no experience there. This usually leads to massive frustration and a lot of wasted effort.

The key is to recognize your areas of weakness and then delegate those areas to organizations that specialize in them. School owners who participate in the NAPMA program are excellent examples of this. They stick to their strengths, which usually center around teaching martial arts, and then they outsource the rest. Since outsourcing allows experts to handle the business-side, its many challenging tasks get done professionally instead of sloppily. In addition, outsourcing makes life as an owner much less stressful, and frees-up twice as much time to spend working with students.

Look at it from the standpoint of the famous 80/20 rule. This time-tested and infallible principle states that 20% of your activities will give you 80% of your results. To that end, it's best to prioritize your work efforts and focus on the 20% of the tasks that will bring you back the highest return. However, in some cases, those high return activities will be beyond your capabilities. I'm talking about activities that you know are really important, but that you're not very good at doing. When you encounter activities like these, it's best not to waste a whole lot of precious time trying to deal with them yourself. Doing so will reduce the amount of productive time you have to spend working on the high return activities that you're actually good at. Make sense?

So remember, rather that trying to be a jack of all trades, stick to your strengths and delegate the rest. You'll be surprised at how much your school will grow.

13: Stick to Your Strengths

Recently I attended the Battle of Atlanta. While I was there, I ran into a former NAPMA member with whom I used to consult. We hadn't spoken in a while, so I asked him how things were going. Right off the bat, I got bad vibes. I could tell something was up.

The gentleman mentioned that he was in the midst of a major restructuring brought on by his own poor judgment and weak management skills. Not long ago, he had built his school up to about 130 students. Everything was going great. But despite NAPMA's advice to seek the assistance of a billing company, he decided to handle the tuition billing on his own. As he described, the results were devastating.

Basically, he lost control of his school. Without the help of a billing company, only nine of his students were still paying for classes. The remaining 93% were taking advantage of his good nature, and simply training for free. Everyone had a list of excuses as to why they couldn't pay for their classes. Being a softie, one by one, the good Sensei let them continue training. Needless to say, this blunder put him right out of business. His school was shut down, and he was forced to shift to a local community center. Ouch!

This gentleman's experience is a classic example of what can happen when you don't stick to your strengths. Let's face it, we all have things we are good at, and things we are not so good at. Smart school owners (smart business owners in general) realize this. That's why they stick to their strengths, and delegate the jobs they are weak at. Conversely, owners who are less experienced in business, think they can run their school as a solo act. They want to be in control of everything, including the things that are outside the realm of their expertise. This is a big mistake that we see occur mainly in the following three areas.

1. Marketing

With all due respect, my daily conversations with school owners around the world validate the fact that the average black belt knows little-to-nothing about marketing… though they will quickly argue this point. Just flip to the martial arts section of the Yellow Pages, and you'll quickly see what I mean.

Most martial arts ads read like self-glorifying resumes. They commonly feature difficult to interpret bullet points such as "Expert in Kuang-Ping Tai Chi". They lead with non-benefit headlines like "Shim Shin Tori-Ryu and Dong P. Kwang Taekwondo". The public has no idea what they're talking about. Even worse are the photos in these ads. You'll see grainy, postage-stamp-sized pictures of a guy leaping over seven people trying to break a board. Others simply go with an intimidating mug shot of the owner, actually thinking it will attract people to their school. We see logos featuring insects, snarling dragons, and rabid animals. These types of ads are designed using black belt eyes instead of market eyes.

The bright spot is that bad marketing can easily be fixed if you delegate that aspect of your business to a company like NAPMA. Each month, NAPMA provides you with professionally designed camera-ready artwork and student newsletters. Expert marketers and designers do all the work for you at a price that anyone can afford. You'll save time and money, enhance your professional image, and get better results. It's a no-brainer.

2. Billing

Many school owners attempt to do their own collections so they can save a few bucks. The problem is that the majority of these owners usually have no background in accounting or money management. The truth is that many of them are poor financial managers, to begin with. For this reason, I've seen numerous owners loose more money than they saved by dabbling in collections. My friend from the Battle of Atlanta will attest to this.

Even more, when you do your own billing, you end up with the additional stress, workload, liability, and time investment. Why not invest these resources into teaching your students? If you don't already use a billing company, I suggest you give it some careful consideration. They're not that expensive, for what you get, and there are plenty to choose from. Just make sure you shop around.

3. Selling

I speak to instructors nearly every day who come right out and admit just how bad they are at sales. I mean, some of these folks feel like a fish out of water trying to sell a two-dollar mouthpiece, let alone a three thousand dollar Black Belt Club program. But they keep limping along with weak sales skills, while their school stays stagnant year after year. That's insanity.

Once again, the solution is to stick to your strengths, and delegate your weak areas. For example, it can be very beneficial to hire a dynamic Program Director to run the sales end of your school. Just make sure the person you select is skilled in the art of selling. Then, let them administrate all the sales pertaining to your enrollments, retail, and renewals. I've seen schools double and triple their growth by doing this. Your results will go up, and your stress will go down.

When it comes to getting expert help with your marketing, billing, and selling, my advice is to spring for the dough. Being frugal is important, but be careful you aren't being penny wise and dollar foolish in the areas that are most instrumental to your school's growth. And always remember... whether you're operating a business, or sparring in the ring, it's best to stick to your strengths.

14: Some Instructors Should Not Own Schools

I was on my way back from Tampa one day when I happened to drive past a friend's karate school. Curiously, I noticed a bunch of parents and kids just standing around in the parking lot. About a half mile down the road, as I peered through three lanes of thick oncoming traffic, I saw something I couldn't believe. It was the owner of the school on roller blades. He was barebacked, frantically skating toward the school about forty-five minutes late. This incident took place right after his car was repossessed (again), and shortly before his school went out of business. It was no surprise when his next school went out of business too.

The black belt I'm referring to is a highly-talented traditional martial artist, an excellent teacher, and an outstanding fighter. To this day, he's still undefeated as a full-contact kickboxer. And he's been blessed with a fantastic personality. However, as he's come to realize, owning a school is not his cup of tea.

My dear, old friend is not alone. I come across many topnotch black belts who consider themselves white belt school owners. A classic example is the full-time owner who struggles to support his family, pay his bills, and save for retirement with a school that never has an active enrollment of more than forty students. It's not that he's independently wealthy, and chooses to have forty students, year after year. The fact is that that's all he is capable of achieving. Eventually, this leads to frustration, stress, attitude challenges, and poverty. So who suffers? Answer: His students, his family, himself, and the image of our industry.

I've noticed that owners like this are mainly weak in the following two areas, which I believe are necessary for success in the world of commercial martial arts.

1. Business Acumen

A commercial martial arts school is a business, and must be operated as such. Unfortunately, some owners are really poor businesspeople. Their strengths do not lie in selling, planning, managing, marketing, organizing, accounting, customer service, writing, motivating, staff training, or personal time-management. So they end up struggling for years, hoping their school will suddenly fill up with students because they have a great hook kick. It doesn't work that way.

2. Leadership Skills

Frankly speaking, some owners are wishy-washy leaders. Leadership is not inherent to their character. As a result, it's difficult for them to attract and keep students and staff. So they have great difficulty building a following. The reality is that these types of owners often make better soldiers, than generals.

While weakness in these key areas can cause a school owner to flop, many other factors can also contribute. For example, some owners are too immature or too incompetent to handle the many responsibilities of a school. In other cases, they don't have the right motivation, knowledge, personality, attitude, or focus to operate a school. Others, in our field, have just been hit in the head too many times.

Regardless of the circumstances, if you're a school owner, and you've tried everything to get your school going, but can't, perhaps ownership is not for you. My suggestion is to think about changing your strategy. Consider teaching for an already-established, successful school owner. You'll get rid of all the headaches that result from owning your own business. At the same time, you can gradually learn the tricks of the trade. Or, you may consider changing careers, and then finding a really great place where you can train like a beast. If you can put your ego aside, you might be much happier with one of these options. Owning a school is definitely not for everyone.

Whatever you decide, just make sure you never skate up on roller blades to unlock the school for kid's class forty-five minutes late. That's really bad for business.

15: KRAs - The First Step to Getting Results

Whether you operate a small school or a large school, it's important to stay focused on your key result areas (KRAs). These are the twenty-percent of the activities that will bring you back eighty-percent of your results. They are the most important tasks you can work on. They are the high return activities that will lead you to big results. Do I have your attention? Let's take a look at six KRAs of an effective martial arts school operator.

KRA 1 - Team Building

A major limiting factor for most school owners is lack of staff. To combat this, I suggest you create a system for team building. Leadership Team is one of the best methods I've ever seen for this, and its the reason why NAPMA has created the Guidance on Leadership Develpment (GOLD Program). We'll hammer out the details of a Leadership Team program later on. But for now, let me just say that your Leadership Team will be your immediate bench strength, and your foundation for future staff.

Guidance On Leadership Development

KRA 2 - Enrolling

Few things can be more important to the health of your school than enrolling new students on a constant basis. Being an expert at diagnostic selling is a key factor, so study this subject hard. In diagnostic sales, you: 1. Ask the right questions. 2. Listen carefully without interruption. 3. Persuasively communicate the benefits of your school. Diagnostic selling is an example of a soft sell. It works perfectly in quality schools where most of the selling is done before the student ever gets to the office.

KRA 3 - Retention

In my opinion, the true secret to establishing a rock solid school is developing high retention. You've got to plug the holes in the bottom of your bucket, whatever they may be. However, the first step towards improving your retention is to know how to calculate your retention. To do this, you take the amount of students you begin the fiscal period with. Add the amount of new students you enrolled during the fiscal period. Then, divide this number into the number of active students your school actually ended the fiscal period with. Most schools operate at a fifty-percent retention rate. Eighty-percent is considered very good. What is yours?

KRA 4 - Quality

The most effective owners I network with are always focused on enhancing the quality of their schools. They're constantly striving to improve their school's look, curriculum, phone skills, enrollment presentation, customer service, staff training, marketing, martial arts skills, testing procedure, etc. Also, it's extremely helpful when you visit other schools. This will give you a barometer by which you can gauge the quality of your own operation.

KRA 5 - Innovation

Some of the most progressive and happiest owners I work with are those who are not afraid to be innovative. They are the owners who are willing to try different approaches, and take calculated risks to make their school a better place. I encourage you to do the same. Remember that the past does not always equal the future.

KRA 6 - Marketing

The quality and quantity of your marketing will have a direct effect on the goals you've set for your school's growth. Regardless of the size of your budget, the best advice I can give you when it comes to marketing is to stay busy, structure your marketing so you constantly get a steady stream of students from a variety of different sources, and make sure it is as professional as possible.

So there you have it. Six basic KRAs for anyone operating a martial arts school. Keep in mind that your list of KRAs can change over time along with you and your school. Also, each individual KRA can increase or decrease in terms of priority, depending upon your school's needs at any given time. The important thing is that both you and your staff members know exactly what your KRAs are, and that you spend the majority of your time working on them. That's the first step towards getting the results you're looking for with your school.

16: What It Takes To Wear the Crown

I'm sure you've heard the old phrase, "It's good to be King." But, is it really? Have you ever stopped to think about what it's like to be "King," or what you have to do to earn the title? What it entails may actually surprise you.

Basically, you can be a "King" at anything you do. It's simply another way of saying that you're considered one of the undisputed leaders in your field. But, let me warn you, it's not easy to achieve this status. Let's take a close look at exactly what it takes to wear the crown.

Aspiring to be the best at what you do is a great goal to have. Personally, I've always believed that it's important to set your goals very high. But I also believe that talk is cheap. In other words, it doesn't matter what you say. It's what you do, that counts. If you want to be number-one... then you've got to prove it.

When it comes to being the best, there is no such thing as luck. You've got to walk your talk. **If you want to be the best, you've got to beat the best. That takes years of hard, hard work, and tremendous focus in the following key areas:**

1. You've Got to Be Hungry For It
Desire is the most important element in becoming numero uno. It doesn't matter if you're a fighter training for a title, or a school owner trying to establish a reputation for excellence. You've got to want it worse than your competition does. If you're not hungrier than the others, there's no way you'll ever become a "King" in your field. Instead, you may end up working for one.

2. You Must Endure the Pain of Sacrifice
No one earns the title of "King" without having made countless sacrifices along the way. That's just the price you pay for it. But most people simply can't handle sacrifice. It's just too tough to constantly do what's difficult and necessary, rather than what's fun and easy. That's why every kingdom has its jesters. I know that sounds cold, but it's true. If it weren't, then everyone would be considered royalty, and we'd all have nothing to strive for.

Sacrifice means starting earlier, working later, and sometimes giving up your weekends. Occasionally it means working while others are having fun. It means managing your time like a world champion body-builder manages his diet. It means taking chances, and being resilient whenever you fail. In today's society, these are tough skills to develop. Only those individuals that are most serious about becoming "King" will be able to endure this kind of continuous pressure. Indeed, sacrifice is the main eliminator of those competing for the crown.

3. You Must Never Become Complacent

In business or competition, there's always somebody waiting to snatch your crown. The quickest way to lose it is to become complacent. That's why it's vital that you maintain the skills and work habits that lead you to success in the first place.

Even more, you have to stay leading-edge. Physically, that means maintaining your martial arts skills, producing great black belts, and staying in shape. Where your mental skills are concerned, it's equally as important to grow. Here, you've got to be willing to invest in new programs and continuing education for both you and your staff. This is essential if you want to avoid being reduced to a "pawn" in a new "King's" court. The moment you become complacent, or take your success for granted, is the moment you'll be dethroned.

Finally, I'd like to point out that devoting your life to becoming the best has both its advantages and disadvantages. Sure, it's great to have prestige, power, wealth, no financial worries, and a feeling of true accomplishment. For many, acquiring faculties such as these represents a dream come true. But, like with all things, there's a trade off. It can be very lonely at the top. In fact, many a "King" has commented that their palace, at times, has seemed like a prison. Also, it can be very stressful having to deal with so much responsibility all the time. Some people are simply not cut-out for that kind of lifestyle. That's why the level of success you want to achieve is purely a personal decision. There is no right or wrong.

So, is it good to be "King," or not? That's a question that only you can answer. However, I strongly encourage you to set your goals as high as possible. There are many rewards that come with success. But always remember that regardless of our business accomplishments or material possessions, we're all "Kings" in our own special way.

17: The Power of Passion

Have you ever wondered how it's possible that some of the wealthiest and most successful people in the world were never formally educated? Or, how others who started out with only minimal knowledge of a particular field went on to revolutionize it? I have, and I've determined that one of the primary reasons for this is **PASSION**.

While the word "passion" has many definitions, we'll be discussing the one that means fervent devotion to a particular cause. In this context, passion gives one the ability to make amazing things happen. Even in situations of incompetence or lack of knowledge, passion has been known to create phenomenal results. A powerful driving force, this single emotion can bring your wildest dreams, visions, and hopes to fruition.

The interesting thing about passion is that it's not like other emotions that can readily be turned on and off. Instead, passion evolves from a deeply rooted inspiration, excitement, or desire that may build up for years before finally exploding to the surface. Once it erupts, an individual will then discover a strong need to achieve, acquire, or fulfill whatever it is that's been brewing inside.

Ultimately, passion will enhance one's endurance, attitude, and drive toward accomplishment. This positively influences performance, and helps one to reach maximum potential. That's why individuals who are truly passionate about something never quit trying, no matter how difficult the circumstances become. Without passion, this level of dedication would be impossible to maintain. Unless one has a genuine, burning desire to achieve a particular goal, the adversity met along the way is almost guaranteed to deter them.

A classic example of the powerful effects of passion can be seen in the NAPMA organization. For starters, the NAPMA team has always had a passionate vision of what we intended to accomplish. Our mission has always been to dramatically increase the amount of people participating in quality martial arts throughout the world. Through the synergies of our monthly support kit, Martial Arts Professional Magazine, the American Council on Martial Arts (ACMA), our popular World Conference, and all of our many turnkey information products, we hit this goal like a sledgehammer.

Second, our hearts are in our work. The NAPMA concept spawned from true martial arts spirit. It's about martial artists helping other martial artists to grow. We launched for all the right reasons and we blazed new trails.

Third, we've gradually built THE best team in the industry, where information products are concerned. When NAPMA was incepted there was just three of us. Today, our team consists of a diverse array of talented professionals that are all extremely passionate about NAPMA's vision.

Fourth, we worked very hard for many years to build the NAPMA organization. We were the ones who gave up karate schools, careers in medicine, and made countless other sacrifices to make it happen. We were the ones who fell asleep at our keyboards in the middle of the night. Hard work has never intimidated us because we're so passionate about what we do.

If you want to run a highly successful martial art school, it's important to have the same level passion. Whether you have it or not, your students and staff probably already realize it. That's because your level of passion shines through in everything you do. It's in your voice when you teach, it's in the way you treat your staff, and it's in your level of enthusiasm when selling the benefits of your school. This being the case, passion is a very hard emotion to fake. Either you have it, or you don't.

I can honestly say that passion is very common in the martial arts field. But sometimes this passion is limited only to specific areas such as teaching, training, competing, managing, etc. However, I have found that the most successful owners are those that are equally passionate in all of these areas, and more.

You see passion gives you a purpose in life, a reason to get out of bed in the morning. When you're passionate about your goals, you're much more likely to achieve them. For a school owner, common goals might be to grow to a certain number of students, reach a certain income level, win certain tournaments, develop multiple locations, etc. With passion, all of these desires can be fulfilled, regardless of what level you're currently at.

But perhaps the most unique effect of true passion is how it allows you to attract new people into your life who are just as passionate as yourself. As they say, like attracts like. It's true. For some reason, we tend to align ourselves with other people who have values, goals, and perceptions similar to our own. Brian Tracy refers to this phenomenon as "the Law of Attraction." It's how great people come together to form great teams in all avenues of life... especially at martial art schools.

I hope this helps you to realize the power of passion. Once you discover what your true passions are, nothing can stand between you and your dreams. So from now on, live each day with passion, and many great things will come your way!

18: I Haven't Worked In Years

According to motivational guru Tom Hopkins, "Work is anything you're doing when you'd rather be doing something else." I guess that's why some of the happiest and most successful people I know are those who do not see what they do for a living as "work." Instead, they see it as their passion.

I'm proud to tell you that many professional martial artists I associate with are classic examples of this. They fell in love with teaching, quit their day job, and opened up a full time school. They've turned their "work" into their play. Now they're living their dream, and they wouldn't want to be doing anything else with their time. It's a wonderful phenomenon when you finally arrive at this place.

On that note, I want to share a little story with you. A few years back I attended one of Ernie Reyes' big black belt promotions. For three days straight, Master Reyes (and his team) pulled together to orchestrate one of the most complex rank exams I'd ever witnessed. On the final day, the exam ran past midnight on a football field, where Master Reyes finally called it a wrap, and officially awarded some 200 triumphant students with their black belts. Everyone, including the staff was exhausted.

The following morning I walked past Master Reyes' school while in route to the airport. As I rubbed my tired eyes, and looked through his storefront window at around 8 a.m. on that crisp Sunday morning, I was amazed to see that he was already back in action. He was out there on the training floor, racing around, helping students learn aerial maneuvers. I remember looking at my watch and thinking… what's he doing here? Doesn't he sleep?

I must admit, Master Reyes' level of dedication and energy totally impressed me and the others I was with. Most instructors would have taken a long vacation after an event of that magnitude. They definitely wouldn't have been back at the school training early the next morning—especially on a Sunday. At that point, it was crystal clear to me that Master Reyes was not "working" anymore. My impression was that he had simply become one with what he does for a living.

Me? I used to "work" too. I was the neighborhood lawn boy. That's how I paid for my first year of martial arts lessons in 1986. I borrowed my grandfather's lawnmower, and cut grass in the hot Florida sun. To me, that was "work" because I didn't enjoy doing it. But now I'm pretty much retired. In fact, I haven't "worked" in about nine years. In my case, I've come to realize that helping the martial arts industry grow is simply what I do now. It's not really my "work" so to speak… it's my passion.

That leads me to the take-home message. When it comes to your occupation, never try to force a square peg into a round hole. If you do not enjoy what you do for a living, then you'll probably be unhappy for as long as you continue to do it. Life's too short to let that happen. As a martial arts school owner, I sincerely hope that you love running a martial arts school. I hope that there is nothing else you'd rather be doing with your time, and that you are 110% committed to your profession. If you truly feel this way, your students will sense it. You will probably be a very fulfilled person, you'll be eager to get out of bed every morning, and, like me, you won't have to "work" anymore.

19: One of the Fastest Ways to Grow

As President of NAPMA, I've resolved to live by the Law of Positive Discontent. Simply put, I'm never 100% satisfied with our progress, but in a healthy and positive way. I believe that there's always room for improvement in everything. Always an opportunity to do a little better, climb a little higher, learn a little more, create something new, or provide our members with a little extra service. We never stop tweaking. To me, that's what success is all about.

When it comes to growing a martial arts school, I recommend you adopt the same philosophy. But in order to improve, you first have to know what changes to make. How do you know this? An easy and effective way is to start visiting other schools. Do this, and you'll learn volumes about yourself and others. You'll enter a brand new world – with every visit – and you'll expose yourself to the information you need to take your school to the next level and beyond.

It should come as no surprise that visiting schools is one of my favorite things to do. I always bring home a treasure chest of knowledge, no matter whose school I visit. As you can see in the photo below, I had the opportunity to tour NAPMA member Steve Stewart's Modern Martial Arts Academy in

Canada. What a highly organized and impressive school! It's conveniently located between an academic school and a church. Is that what they mean by location, location, location?

Steve teaches over five hundred students, and his school is loaded with unique features such as the video camera system that allows him to observe each of his training areas at all times. I thought that was a great idea for increasing safety and decreasing liability. As long as you're receptive to new ideas, you'll bring home a "golden nugget" such as this one every time.

But the best part of visiting other schools is that it creates a barometer by which you can gauge the success of your own operation. In other words, you have to have a standard to measure your own progress against. A marker, if you will. Sometimes you'll walk into someone's school, and the "eureka phenomenon" will occur. Jackpot! You'll bring home a whole satchel full of "golden nuggets" that could change the very way you run your school forever. Sometimes, you'll learn exactly how not to do something. That, too, is extremely valuable information. In other cases, you'll validate what you're already doing. A little reassurance is sometimes just what the doctor ordered. But, before any of this can happen, you've got to get out there, and invest the resources necessary to make it so.

In the recent past, I've had the pleasure of visiting Dr. Kum Sung's school in New Jersey, Tiger Shulman's school in New York, Joon P. Choi's school in Ohio, Cesar Ozuna's school in Florida, and Ernie Reyes' school in California just to name a few. Plus, when I was in Germany recently I stopped into NAPMA member Oliver Drexler's school, which is amazingly large for his population. It was very interesting to see NAPMA posters, ads, and management ideas translated into German. Did I mention that Oliver teaches a great Little Ninjas class?

The take-home message is that we don't know what we don't know, and decisions can be very easy to make when we don't have all the facts. When you visit other schools, you fix this. Only then does it make sense to apply the Law of Positive Discontent. So I hope that I've inspired you to begin visiting other schools. There's no doubt that it's one of the best things you can do to broaden your horizons, and one of the fastest ways to grow your school. That I guarantee!

20: Eight Ways to Boost Your Gross

Want to heat-up your school's gross—FAST? The key is to target specific revenue-related areas of your business, develop an action plan for improvement, and then focus on it like a laser. Here now is a list of eight simple suggestions to get you started!

1. Raise Your Tuition
If you're still charging fifty or sixty bucks per month for lessons...TWENTY KNUCKLES! Make that twenty knuckles in the parking lot, on glass! The average price of tuition in the US is somewhere around one hundred dollars per month. So if you haven't raised your rates in the last decade or two, I suggest you do so (incrementally) for all new students coming in. Just be sure you are delivering a service that is equal to your fee.

2. Host More Special Events
Did I ever tell you about the time that I caught Chicken Pox at one of our school lock-ins? Hey, it was worth it, 'cause we got the gross up that month. Seriously though, if you're not doing at least one special event per month, your gross is not as high as it could be. How about birthday parties, holiday shopping sprees, weapons seminars, movie nights, awards banquets, lock-ins, celebrity guest instructors, etc? I suggest you conduct at least one special event per month, and post your calendar of events one-year in advance so students can make plans to attend.

3. Collect More Tuition Up-Front
Some instructors firmly believe that you must collect a student's total contract value sooner rather than later. For example, if a student enrolls for a year they try to collect all the tuition in the first couple of months. Or, they try to get the student cashed-out upon enrolling. One reason they do this is so the school gets paid the full contract amount even if the student drops out. While other instructors have philosophical challenges with this strategy, the bottom line is that collecting more tuition up front will indeed raise your gross.

4. Increase Your Enrollments
Increasing your enrollments will obviously boost your gross. But first you must increase the amount of new student leads you are receiving. You do this through tons of clever marketing. Yes, marketing is the key. To that end, are you staying busy with holiday gift certificates promotions, VIP passes, demos, Buddy Days, print ads, web marketing, telemarketing, referral contests, direct

mailers, academic school talks, etc? The point is that more marketing creates more leads. With more leads you'll generate more enrollments, and ultimately increase your gross.

5. Pump-up Your Product Sales

Now I know this sounds simple, but if you actually focus on selling more products in your school, you probably will. I've seen schools increase their product sales literally by several thousand percent simply by putting some extra effort into it. Are you offering nutritional supplements, specialty items for Little Ninjas, healthy hydration products, apparel, or a diverse selection of equipment? Has your staff been trained on suggestive selling? Are you making announcements in class, featuring products each month, reselling used equipment, handing out catalogs, etc? C'mon, you know this stuff. My goal here is simply to remind you to take action!

6. Diversify Your Services

Many schools that have successfully increased their gross have done so by offering additional services such as preschool classes, after school martial arts, CDT, Krav Maga, Kanarek's F.I.G.H.T System, summer camps, the UBC, tai chi, fitness kickboxing, etc. Any of these programs can bring more tuition dollars, referrals, and product sales into your school. You just have to choose the alternate profit centers that make sense for you.

7. Conduct More Renewals

Many top-grossing schools conduct a high percentage of membership renewals. Black Belt Club and Masters Club programs can have a huge financial impact, especially if you can get ten to fifteen percent of your students to cash out. So the strategy with renewals is to first systemize this area of your school, and then simply start conducting more of them. The initial investments, increased monthly tuition, and cash outs you receive will do wonders for improving your gross.

8. Maximize Initial Investments

Through consulting, I've learned that some schools do not ask for initial investments. Unless they know something I don't know, this is a mistake. Look at it this way… if you're enrolling just ten students per month, and they each put down only $199…well, you do the math. Oh, and add in your renewal initial investments too, at say $249 each. This translates to big bucks! Collecting initial investments and/or collecting them in greater dollar amounts is a fast and easy way to accelerate your cash flow, and give your gross a tremendous shot in the arm.

21: No Guts, No Glory

According to fellow martial artist Brian Tracy, "Your heart should be in your throat at least once a day." But what does the supreme guru of all that makes sense mean by this? Well, he's simply implying that in order to get ahead in this world, you've got to be willing to take risks.

Ask nearly anyone who's successful in any area, and they'll tell you that Mr. Tracy's mantra is right on the money. In order to climb up the ladder of success, you must have the courage to venture. That means being willing to take certain chances in life. This is mandatory if you plan to grow personally, professionally, or financially.

However, taking risks can be very difficult for some people. If this describes you, don't feel bad. Feeling comfortable with risk is something that you have to condition yourself to over time. That's because risk taking often requires that you step out of your comfort zone, go against something you may have previously been taught, or do what your instincts tell you not to do. Getting yourself to accept behavioral changes such as these, is not naturally easy. It's a mentality that must be developed.

Psychologically, when we're afraid of something, it's usually because we don't fully understand it. For many people, risk falls into this category. Those who don't understand it, are typically scared of it. So they avoid taking risks, and are overly conservative throughout their lives. Consequently, this causes them to grow at a snail's pace. On the other hand, those that understand risk, often use it to their advantage. This places them on the fast track to success, in many areas of life. But in order to maximize your return on risk, knowledge of the following three elements is key:

1. Risk Tolerance
When acclimatizing yourself to risk taking, the first step is to know just how much risk you're willing to absorb. The best way to figure this out is to ask yourself "How much am I willing to lose?" Once you determine that, then you've established your risk tolerance. But be honest with yourself when it comes to this. A risk can go either way, regardless of how great the odds may appear. The last thing you want is to find yourself in a predicament if something were to go wrong. As the age old rule states: "Never gamble with something that you can't afford to lose."

2. The Risk-Reward Ratio

Understanding the risk-reward ratio can really bring to light the importance of taking risks. This rule states, the greater the level of risk, the greater the level of reward." But, keep in mind that the opposite of this also holds true. There's a direct relationship between the level of risk and likelihood of loss. That's why it's so important that you learn to analyze risk factors, and take calculated risks that are based upon facts.

3. Calculated Risk

Since risks and rewards are generally in direct proportion to one another, learning how to use risk to your advantage is critical. The key is to take risks that are calculated, not impulsive. A calculated risk is one that results from lots of deliberation and careful thought. Here, all aspects of the risk taking decision are weighed out in advance. This method helps you make educated decisions, thereby reducing your chances for failure.

As a martial arts consultant, I speak with many school owners who are afraid to take any business risks at all. That's ironic since these are the same individuals that spar, break boards, and wield razor sharp weapons, without hesitation. Oh, you wanna whack an apple out of my mouth with your Nunchaku? Sure, no problem." Yet, when it comes to other types of risks, the same bunch is notoriously bashful.

Common examples of risks for martial arts professionals include adjusting curriculums, opening multiple locations, breaking away from certain traditions, leaving associations, switching billing companies, trying new marketing strategies, and investing. Though many school owners passionately complain about how unhappy they are because of issues such as these, they tend to procrastinate when it comes to doing something about them. That's unfortunate because most of these so-called risks, once taken, end up working out for the best.

In conclusion, risk taking can be very positive when it's handled responsibly. That means analyzing the facts, making logical decisions, and being willing to take certain chances. By the way, doing this will definitely put your heart in your throat. But that's okay. As martial artists, we can relate...no guts, no glory!

22: Your Dreams CAN Come True

At the age of nine, my eyesight was already so bad that I was forced to start wearing glasses. As a kid growing up, that was a real drag. For years, I was called four-eyes, and bullies constantly teased me.

Then, at the age of fourteen, I began taking martial arts lessons. Wearing my glasses to class each night quickly became a nuisance. I would sweat so much, while working out in the sweltering Florida heat, that the heavy frames soon created a rash on my nose and cheeks. Plus, it was nearly impossible to throw spin kicks or spar with them on. Realizing this, I got rid of my glasses, and switched to contact lenses.

Due to a nasty astigmatism in both eyes, I had to wear a special type of lenses called Torics. These contacts were real expensive, but thank God for them! They allowed me to train extremely hard, and fight for many years with relatively few challenges. Though they were constantly dirty, scratchy, or out of focus, I was very grateful for them. Without those lenses, I wouldn't have been able to tell the difference between Kathy Long and Joe Lewis from five feet away.

But, all of that is over now. After wearing glasses and contacts for most of my life, I'll never have to depend on corrective eyewear again. That's because I experienced a "miracle" called LASIK (Laser Assisted Insitu Keratomileusis). LASIK is one of the most common and safest types of laser eye surgeries available today. Millions of people with bad eyesight are having it done. That's because LASIK actually restores vision, permanently.

Believe it or not, I now have natural 20/20 vision in both eyes. The most amazing part of it all is that the surgery took only a few minutes, and was completely painless. Within a few moments after the procedure, I had crystal clear vision as I walked to my car, and went home. I'm still amazed by this. For me, it's like an impossible dream that somehow came true.

But, there's a much deeper reason I'm writing about this experience, other than to inform you about my new improved vision. The lesson to be learned from all of this is that no matter how outrageous or impossible your dreams may seem, there's always a chance they'll come to life. This is especially possible in today's world, where dreams have a better-than-ever chance of materializing. On this note, let's zoom in on two types of dreams.

1. Intangible Dreams

First, there are the dreams over which you have no control. Let's refer to them as "intangible" dreams. An example of an intangible dream, for me, was getting my vision restored. I always imagined that this might someday be possible, but there really wasn't anything I could do to turn that dream into a reality.

With intangible dreams, you just have to stay positive, and have hope. But, look at it this way. We live in the most advanced and amazing time in the history of our world. Technology is advancing so fast that it's hard to even keep up with it. That which is totally impossible today, may become easily achievable tomorrow. Just remember to always keep your dreams alive, have patience, and learn to recognize dream-fulfilling opportunities when they finally present themselves.

2. Tangible Dreams

Second, there are the types of dreams over which you have direct control. Let's refer to them as "tangible" dreams. Examples are: What you want your school to be like in five years; how many students you want to impact with your teachings; what kind of lifestyle you want to lead, etc. Tangible dreams are the kind that you, yourself, can make come true. In fact, the outcome of dreams like these are, indeed, controlled by you.

In business, especially, nearly any dream can become a reality if you're willing to work hard enough to achieve it. Here, you can accomplish seemingly impossible goals with the right amount of effort, dedication, and patience. Just realize that every single decision you make, on a daily basis, will either take you closer to, or farther from, your dreams. That's a key point. Like I said, the achievement of tangible dreams is strictly up to you.

As I sit here, writing this book with no corrective eyewear, I'm living proof that dreams can come true. My new 20/20 vision is a perfect example. I only hope this true story inspires you to stay focused on any aspirations you may have for yourself and your school. But, most importantly, I hope that I've inspired you to dream the impossible dream.

23: Your Beliefs Will Shape Your Future

Would you like to create your own destiny, take control of your future, and increase the quality of your life? If so, you've got to start believing in yourself today. You've got to think like a winner, and eliminate any thoughts or actions that might hold you back. You've got to imagine you already are where you want to be, and that nothing could make you fail. You've got to create your own positive self-fulfilling prophecies.

As it pertains to management, Robert Merton conceptualized the notion of the self-fulfilling prophecy in 1957. It occurs when "a false definition of the situation evokes a new behavior which makes the original false conception come true." Translation—as a school owner, when you set an expectation, even if it isn't accurate, your actions tend to be consistent with that expectation. Often, the result is that the expectation comes true.

For example, if you constantly tell yourself that you can't grow your school, then your school will probably not grow. "Argue for your weaknesses, and they're yours," says world-renowned psychologist Dr. Stephen Covey. However, the reverse of this also holds true, and it's just as powerful. Make yourself believe that you are going to succeed at whatever you do, and you will greatly increase your chances for success.

Ultimately, we become what we think about most. In other words, our thoughts become our realities. That's why it is so critically important to concentrate on your strengths, opportunities, and potentials rather than your weaknesses, failures, and limitations. Unfortunately, some owners tend to focus on the negative way too much. They convince themselves that they can't succeed, and as a result they typically don't. In my experience as a consultant, here are some common examples of what I mean.

Consultant: If you create a Black Belt Club, it will help you enhance your retention.

Owner: Black Belt Club is a good idea, but I just know it won't work in my school.

Consultant: If you begin a Leadership Team, you'll start to develop staff members.

Owner: Tried it already. No one wanted to be on my Leadership Team.

Consultant: If you host special events, you'll increase your revenue.

Owner: Special events never work for me. My students don't support them.

Consultant: Have you ever considered offering Fitness Kickboxing?

Owner: Uh-uh. That won't work in my area. The people around here are unique.

Consultant: Have you ever considered joining NAPMA, since you're having difficulty breaking past 50 students?

Owner: I would, but I just don't have the time to use the materials.

Ah, yes...argue for your weaknesses, and they will be yours. Owners like this are difficult to consult with indeed. They operate with a victim's mentality, and their schools are almost always less fruitful than they would like them to be. They convince themselves that nothing works for them. Then they gradually create the evidence to support their claims, which proves to the world that they were right all along. But, worst of all, they blame others for their problems, when the real culprit is the man in the mirror. This is a self-fulfilling prophecy of the worst kind.

On the other hand, I work with so many highly successful school owners that do exactly the opposite. They focus their mental and physical energies on positive thoughts and actions. They think big, not small. They have a great attitude and lots of self-confidence. They make goals instead of excuses. They're proactive, not reactive. They're highly motivated, future-focused, and optimistic. This overall attitude creates positive self-fulfilling prophecies as evidenced by their many accomplishments.

So the take-home message is that you have the power to influence your own future. First, set positive expectations for yourself and your school. Next, you've got to truly believe in those expectations so your daily actions and decisions will begin to reflect them. Then, as if by magic, your expectations will come true.

24: Martial Arts is a Personality Driven Business

There is no question in my mind that martial arts is a personality driven business. Your success will not be determined by what style you teach. It doesn't matter how many trophies you've won. You can call yourself a second-degree black belt or an eighth-degree. It's not about whether you use contracts or EFTs. You can be black, white, yellow, or green. You can be a girl or a guy, young, or old. When it comes to your success as an instructor, the quality of your persona is what will make the difference.

The fact is that some instructors happen to have the right blend of charisma, leadership skills, and personality to create and keep students. For some, these attributes just come naturally. This allows them to have high retention without having a "magical" method for keeping students. They have strong enrollment numbers though their sales skills aren't the best. Students support their special events in droves. In short, they seem to have a knack for successfully selling others on all that they say and do. Other instructors fail at this, big time.

For example, you can give Instructor-A and Instructor-B the exact same business system. You can give them the exact same demographics, marketing tools, sales training, resources, and curriculum. You can create a situation where all factors are equal. In the end, Instructor-A may flourish, and Instructor-B may flop.

I've seen countless examples of this throughout the years. In fact, I've personally dealt with instructors who were extremely talented martial artists, but their students rarely stuck around past green belt. I've consulted with instructors who have had beautiful schools in prime locations, yet they couldn't generate enough students to keep their doors open. I've seen instructors with a college background in sales and marketing go out of business. Why? Usually, it's not because their marketing, curriculum, location, or martial arts skills are so much worse than everyone else's. Typically, it's their interpersonal skills that hold them back. They simply do not have that magnetic, charismatic, personality that allows them to create and maintain a following. They're like a meal that's missing a key ingredient. It looks great on your plate, but proves disappointing to your taste buds.

In my experience, these types of instructors often suffer from a combination of character deficiencies. For example, they may come across as boring because they lack quality presentation skills. Other instructors can demonstrate their techniques backwards and forwards, but they have a real problem conveying the information to others. Some people are simply not good teachers. Then there are those instructors that are clueless when it comes to pushing the right hot buttons on the deck or in the office. Selling is 90% emotional, so naturally these types consistently end up with poor results. In addition, some instructors wouldn't recognize an opportunity if it hook kicked them right in the head. So their competitors end up eating their lunch. The list goes on.

So what's the solution for an instructor with a personality deficit? For starters, I have to remind you that it is always best to match the skills of an individual with the requirements of a job. That's one of the fundamental rules of delegation. You don't want to put someone in a position that requires a skill set that they do not have. If we're talking about a Chief Instructor or a Program Director, you want to make sure that they are energetic, charismatic, and professional. They should have excellent presentation, communication, listening, and leadership skills. They should be friendly, courteous, well groomed, and likeable. If you choose people to fill roles such as these and they do not have the appropriate skill sets, then you are probably setting the system up for failure.

Also, keep in mind that it may take a little time to determine what an individual's true skill set actually consists of. They may simply need some fine-tuning in a particular area. Perhaps, they're a diamond in the rough. One of the easiest things you can do to discover this, and possibly inject some personality skills into a personality-weak instructor, is to find them an outstanding role model. Let them see, hear, and experience what a personality-rich instructor brings to the table. If some personality doesn't rub off on them, then you know you do not have the right person for the job. You just have to give someone a chance to improve before you make the decision to replace him or her.

As much as it saddens me to say it, some instructors will never make it in the martial arts business unless they improve critical personality-related skills such as the aforementioned. Clearly, there's much more to running a successful school than just having quality support information and excellent martial arts skills. Image, panache, charisma, heart, personality, and strong leadership skills all weigh in to make a martial arts school complete.

25: Charisma - The Keystone Trait

I have found that a martial arts instructor's level of success usually parallels his level of charisma. That's because when an instructor has charisma, all school-related programs and procedures just seem to fall into place easier. But when an instructor is missing it, running a school can seem like an uphill battle. Indeed, I'm convinced that charisma is a quality that often separates the best from the rest in business.

As I stated in the previous passage, I firmly believe that martial arts is a personality driven business. People usually get involved and stay involved with the training to the level they are motivated by the instructor. Also, the lessons are not a commodity product, or a guaranteed sale like fast food. So a school's success depends largely upon the instructor's ability to inspire students, and keep them interested in the lessons. Charisma is the keystone trait that allows that to happen naturally.

By definition, charisma is a unique personal power belonging to those exceptional individuals capable of securing the allegiance of large numbers of people. Some sources define it as the ability to command, inspire and motivate others. But what is it about these people that allows this to occur? In my opinion, it's not one thing that makes a person charismatic. It's a whole bunch of things.

For instance, charismatic people generally possess the following talents:

1. They have superb communication skills. They are able to articulate complex messages clearly and confidently to others.

2. They have very strong listening skills. This makes others feel comfortable and accepted when in their presence. We'll detail this topic in the very next section.

3. They are persuasive communicators. Using the right blend of words and timing they are able to persuade others to see it as they see it.

4. They have strong beliefs and are often looked upon as visionaries. Others find them interesting and look upon them as a leader.

5. They have the ability to build rapport with others quickly and easily. Once again, this makes them likeable and helps them to build a following.

Knowing this, wouldn't you agree that charisma is a trait that could be beneficial to all martial arts instructors?

Clearly, instructors that possess charisma are well positioned to grow their schools. They just have a certain charm about them that causes people to join more frequently and with less hesitation. Also, charismatic instructors retain students for longer periods of time. That's because their students aren't bored by the instruction. They're motivated, inspired, and excited by it. In short, charisma helps instructors to create and keep students.

On the other hand, instructors that lack charisma can cause their school to suffer. These types typically complain that nothing works for them. They say they can't get a Leadership Team started, no one shows up for demo team practice, staff members keep leaving, people won't enroll, nobody supports special events, etc., etc., etc. When they're done whining, they usually blame it all on their area. But in reality, they are the cause. Their personality is usually too silly, too serious, too boring, too pushy, or too lackadaisical. Often, they are uninteresting, non-motivating, and long-winded. Instructors like this unintentionally run people off, and end up with one of those infamous "stuck-in-a-rut schools" for years.

From a purely business perspective, an instructor's background in the arts may offer little reward without charisma. I say that because I often chat with successful school owners who are not champions, high-ranking blackbelts, martial arts veterans, or even the greatest practitioners in the world. But the one thing they do have going for them is their ability to "sell" a vision of the martial arts. They have the knack for getting people to "buy" into what they are offering. In other words, they have charisma, which garners trust, and gives them believability. This one essential quality allows certain instructors to build and maintain a strong following of students regardless of their location, economy, business plan, or style.

Furthermore, many charismatic instructors are able to operate successfully even though they often deviate from conventional martial arts business ideals. For example, some instructors purposely teach grueling classes yet have hundreds of students that keep coming back for more. Others maintain large schools even though they have no Black Belt Club or Leadership Team. Some peak-performing studios are run like temples. Others are like martial arts fitness centers. Many use contracts, while others use EFT's, both, or none. Style, too, is irrelevant when it comes to success. I could go on and on. The point is that regardless of how they run their school, a charismatic instructor usually has a better shot at making it work.

26: We Have Two Ears and One Mouth for a Reason

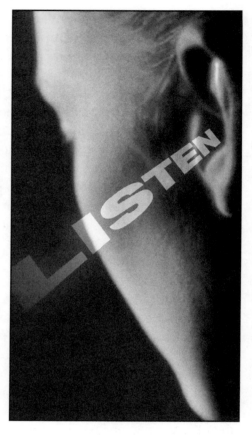

Have you ever found yourself "pretend listening" to someone? As they rambled on, you were off in your own little world, imagining you were Bruce Lee, repeatedly spin-hook-kicking an army of defenseless, pint-sized, karate guys about the head. G'aw head, admit it. When that someone was finally finished speaking, all you could remember hearing was *Bawds don't hit back*. Okay, Bruce—snap out of it!

As martial artists, we spend countless hours practicing our forms and fighting skills. As school-age children, we were grilled on developing communication skills such as reading, writing, and speaking. But what about listening? How much time does the average person spend practicing their listening skills? Answer: Almost none.

For about the first twenty-five years of my life, I was a poor listener. Then, I realized that when you're speaking, you're reciting that which you already know. But when you're listening, you're learning. I heard this many times throughout my life from my mentors...but as usual I wasn't listening. Then one day I was ready to hear it and a light bulb went off. (Blink.)

With all due respect, most people I encounter are not very good listeners. They listen with the intent to reply, not to hear and understand. Instead of truly listening to what others are saying, they're either talking over them, or mentally preparing a response. Or they're pretend listening (yeah, uh-huh, right). So they end up missing important chunks of conversation.

Also, the tendency of many is to force feed their own views, opinions, and experiences down the throats of others when they should be listening. Rather than engage in equal conversation, they prefer to smack the other person over the head with a copy of their autobiography. You go to speak, and right away they cut you off with their own version of your story (a favorite technique of control freaks). That quickly becomes frustrating, not to mention rude.

Ah, yes… learning to listen can be quite challenging, indeed. But the pursuit of self-mastery never ends, and practicing strong listening skills is a key element to focus on for both personal and professional reasons alike.

For example, strong listening skills are very important to the process of enrolling and renewing students at your school. As you'll read in Section 29, asking good questions, and then attentively listening for clues that help you close a sale, is the essence of effective selling. That's why top salespeople spend as much as 80% of their time listening, and only 20% speaking. On the other hand, amateur salespeople do more talking than listening. They think that selling is telling, but it's not.

Now, here's a tip that will help you become a top-level manager. One of the greatest needs that humans have is to feel understood. And one of the best ways to make someone feel understood is to listen to them, empathetically and without interruption. Try this with your staff members, and you'll be amazed at the results. Make them feel understood, and you'll dramatically increase the moral authority you have over them. Though you'll always have the final decision, they'll feel important because you allowed them to contribute. That translates to happier employees who are more receptive to your leadership.

Okay, Bruce, now listen-up. When you're interacting with students, employees, friends, or family, make a conscious effort to engage in active listening. Try not to be a pretend listener like I was. Don't shoot their ideas down before they're finished speaking. Avoid cutting them off in mid-sentence. Resist the urge to complete their words for them because *I can already see where you're going with this.* Instead, have patience, and truly listen. That shouldn't be too tough considering you have two ears and only one mouth.

27: Give Me Racehorses!

In this passage, I do not plan to mince words. I've drawn my whip, and I plan to jockey home a management message that I'm extremely passionate about. I'm referring to a topic that's crucial to the long-term success or failure of your school. That topic is employee selection.

For starters, let's compare two types of employees: the "racehorse" and the "plow-horse." Racehorse employees are lean n' mean, active, confident, ambitious, and fast. Yes, very fast. Plus, they're highly competitive and extremely results-oriented. They do not suffer from "analysis paralysis." Au contraire! They need to run. So they make decisions quickly, and they attack. They were built for speed, and it's practically impossible to hold them back. They're powerful. Hence, the racehorse employee is well equipped to take your school to the next level and beyond.

Now let's compare the typical plow-horse type employee. They're slow, complacent, and unproductive. They lack creativity, ambition, and drive. They take their sweet time on every assignment, and put forth the minimum level of effort. In other words, they coast, and make excuses for their weak results. Look up Parkinson's Law in the dictionary, and you'll see their picture. The sad truth is that no matter how much you like them, no matter how nice they are, they will do little or nothing to grow your school.

On this note, I've found that the best schools have the best teams running them. They employ a team of racehorses. For example, in successful schools the Chief Instructor is almost always dynamic, charismatic, and motivational. He or she teaches classes that leave students euphoric, and wanting more. Their leadership skills are strong, and their martial arts skills are brow raising. They're innovative and they work tirelessly to ensure high levels of student retention. Likewise, such schools typically employ a world class Program Director that is, in a word, sharp. He or she is pumped, articulate, and organized. Their people skills are a nine or ten, on a scale of ten. They're autonomous, efficient, productive, and focused. On top of that, they're a "black belt" at sales. Translation: they get results, and they get them consistently. I could go on and describe every employee in a topnotch school, but I think you get the idea. These people are peak performers. They do not work like plow-horses.

Just in case you haven't gathered, my idea of running a business places a heavy emphasis on racehorse type employees. I'm looking for a small group of highly efficient, highly paid individuals who can each do the work of five plow-horses with an even greater degree of competence. I'm not interested in Mr. or Mrs. Go-Nowhere. I'm looking for someone who wants to grow. Someone who wants to win the derby, if you will. Granted, these types of employees are difficult to find and they're expensive. But they do exist, and they're worth every penny you pay them. Just be sure to structure their employment arrangements carefully. As I said earlier, racehorses need to run. You don't want them to gallop off into the sunset, and at the same time you don't want them to throw a saddle on you. So keep your guard up.

Lastly, what do you do if you have a plow-horse or two working at your school? My advice is simple. De-hire them. Let them go graze on somebody else's payroll. Don't get me wrong, putting a plow-horse out to pasture can be a difficult decision in some cases, but it's nothing personal. Once you've done all that you can possibly do to make a racehorse out of them, but can't, you've got a serious decision to make. A decision that's often considered taboo among "white belt" managers. You've got to decide to carry them forever, or let them go. I suggest you replace them with a racehorse.

That having been said, would you rather have racehorses or plow-horses on your payroll? You're the one that has to cut the checks, so it's up to you. Me? Give me racehorses!

28: Dialing-Up on Phone Skills

With NAPMA being the world's largest professional martial arts organization, I'm on the phone constantly. It's such a great experience when the person answering my call has excellent phone skills. I'm referring to the kind of person that's friendly, enthusiastic, patient, courteous, and professional. Employees like these make me feel important. They give me the impression that the school they represent is as topnotch as they are. Such individuals immediately make me feel welcome, at ease, impressed.

On the contrary, many schools I contact allow employees with horrible phone skills to answer their phones. Typically, their tone conveys that they're in a hurry, and that my call is inconveniencing them. Their voice and delivery indicates that they are stressed out or overwhelmed. Sometimes, they are more than just curt—they're flat out rude. I can't help but feel that they're a reflection of the rest of their school's employees and customer service policies. Ultimately, front-end-people like these can end up costing you a fortune... in lost business!

In my opinion, the person you have answering your phone should have expert phone skills. Nothing less will do. At NAPMA, we've actually de-hired receptionists that couldn't be trained to our standards. I tell you this because I want you to realize I'm as serious as a heart attack when it comes to answering a telephone properly. To that end, here are some of my best tips for developing phenomenal phone skills.

Sound Inviting
The tone of your voice should project warmth, care, sincerity, courtesy, and appreciation. Make the caller feel glad they called.

Master Standard Lines
Mastering standard lines like "Thank you for calling USA Karate, my name is Rob, how may I help you?" is a thousand times better than winging it, or answering the phone with something brash like "Karate school!" Also, keep in mind that role-playing is one of the best ways to fine-tune phone skills, and develop a smooth delivery.

Here I am performing on our USA Karate Television series, which aired for over
a decade in the Tampa Bay area.

That's me destroying five boards with a fighting jump turn kick
on my second-degree black belt exam.

For my third-degree black belt exam and promotion, I shattered some baseball bats
with my shin. What was I thinking?

A popular image that's been seen around
the world, I'm blitzing forward against
my instructor John Graden.

As a professional martial artist,
my specialty was kickboxing.

My third degree exam had two ambulance calls. One of which took place during this grueling three mile run. Here I am crossing the finish line with a black eye and a severely swollen foot from side kicking another fighter in the elbow right before the run. Ouch! We really earned our belts.

In the early days I used to coordinate the stuffing of NAPMA's monthly membership kits. Then, we'd deliver them to the post office in our own cars. We've come a long way!

One of the things I enjoy most is conducting seminars on the subject of effective martial arts school operations.

Creating the nationwide Coca-Cola program to bring healthy hydration products to the martial arts industry was a significant milestone in my career. Here, National Account Executive, Adrienne Johnson, is presenting me with a lead crystal Coke bottle in recognition of our new partnership.

In the trenches, as a Program Director
for nine years at *USA Karate*, I learned volumes
about selling martial arts memberships.

During my career at NAPMA, I've had the honor
of interacting with superstar personalities such
as Arnold Schwarzenegger, Chuck Norris,
Bernard Kerik, Pat Morita and a host of others.

As NAPMA's Public Relations spokesperson for many years, I've conducted interviews on the
martial arts with media sources ranging from Time Magazine to video documentaries.

Follow the Two Ring Rule

My rule of thumb is to answer the phone after no more than two rings. Don't keep the caller waiting any longer than necessary.

Answer the Phone Calmly

Doesn't it make you feel awkward when someone frantically takes your call? Or, when they rapidly blurt out a line like "Thankyouforcallingcanlhelpyou?!" followed by a huge stress-related sigh? Avoid sounding like you're in a hurry, even if you are. Don't penalize the caller because you're busy or under pressure.

Speak Like a Professional

Avoid asking questions like, "Who are you?" or making statements like "Gimme that number again." Instead, "May I have your name, sir?" and "Can you please repeat your phone number, ma'am?" is a much more professional approach.

Take Accurate Messages

It's embarrassing when you return a call from Bill, and his name is really Phil; or when you can't return a client's call because you don't have all the correct digits in their phone number. Always listen carefully, and repeat the information back to the caller, to ensure accuracy.

Proper Physiology Projects Enthusiasm

Your voice will always sound more enthusiastic to the caller if you sit up straight, and smile when you are speaking. This will also help you sound happy, as opposed to monotone and bored. Your goal is to always create an image for the caller that the sun is shining over your school, even if it's raining.

Be Courteous

Few things irritate me more than when you ask to speak to someone, and the receptionist just clicks a button without saying a word. Example: Can I speak to Mr. Smith. CLICK! A better approach would be, "Yes, sir. If you'll hold one moment, I'll be glad to see if he's available." Don't forget to use common courtesies just because the other person isn't standing in front of you.

29: Solve Your Students' Pain with Diagnostic Selling

L et's discuss one of the most vital functions of any school. I'm referring to the most misunderstood and scary part of the business for most owners. The subject is selling. Ironically, all schools rely on sales to stay in business. Without sales, you couldn't survive.

As a Program Director myself for many years, one of the most valuable sales skills I ever learned was Diagnostic Selling. Sound complicated? It's not. Diagnostic Selling is very basic. It occurs when you assume the role of a consultant, and are there to "help" the student instead of "sell" the student. You are viewed as a professional consultant of the martial arts, and your mission is to facilitate a decision that will make a positive difference in someone's life. You are NOT viewed as a slick salesperson out to make a fast commission. Diagnostic Selling is an example of soft selling, and it's based out of integrity. That's why it works so well at a martial arts school.

There are 3 aspects of Diagnostic Selling that I want you to remember.

1. Ask the Right Questions
This is extremely important to the Diagnostic Sales process. The key here is to gather information. You want to find out as much as you can about what the other person wants or needs. Or, you might try to sell them the wrong way. You may try to sell them the wrong thing.

For instance, in a typical phone call you might be asked, "What style do you teach?" Most owners would answer with an explanation of their style and why it's so effective. When this happens you're getting off track. Your job is NOT to spend time answering questions that are unrelated to the real issue, which is getting the caller happily involved in your school. Your job is to understand the other person's needs. In fact, you should answer the question "What style do you teach?" with something like, "Is there a particular style you're interested in?" Ah ha! Now you've got the chance to learn something about that person and their interests. Make sense?

Like a good engineer you have to understand what forces and stresses are at work before you can build a bridge. Questions like "What is it about martial arts that interests you?" or "Tell me a little bit about your son...is he shy, or is he real outgoing?" are the types of questions that help you determine the stresses. Just remember to be very relaxed and very conversational. That's one of the keys to making this process work effectively.

2. Listen for Clues Without Interrupting

This is often a very weak area among many sales people. They don't like to listen, instead they like to do all of the talking. The problem is that when you're talking you're repeating that which you already know. That doesn't help you when you're trying to make a sale. It actually hurts you. What will help you is if you resist the urge to speak while the other person is trying to answer YOUR questions. It is imperative that you let the other person tell you what they are looking for without interruption. Remember the phrase: Telling is not Selling.

3. Persuasively Communicate the Benefits

This is the final stage. So far, you have asked the prospect all the right questions. You've listened very attentively to what they need and want. You've carefully narrowed it down so there is no doubt as to how you should proceed and what "hot buttons" you should push. The other person feels comfortable with you because you've taken the time to listen to what THEY want instead of trying to tell them what YOU want. You've aligned with them. Now that you've gotten this far, you have permission to start selling.

At this point, it's your job to explain to the prospect exactly how your school can help them to achieve their goals. They just told you what their goals are. Now, as a consultant, it's up to you to take the information you gathered, and PROVE to them that your school can help them to get what they want. Did you know that selling is 90% emotional? Therefore, you must learn how to draw emotion out of other people. That's one of the main objectives of Diagnostic Selling.

Finally, I want to mention that Diagnostic Selling should not be the only technique in your arsenal. You still have to be an expert at all basic sales techniques. Also, if you do not have superior telephone skills, a professional-looking school, and a solid benefit-oriented introductory lesson, you will greatly diminish your chances of being successful with Diagnostic Sales. Most of the selling should be done before you ever get to the office. So the concept of Diagnostic Selling is really just a foundation for you to work from.

30: How to Increase Results and Decrease Stress with the Right Program Director

It's important to realize that there are two separate halves to operating a commercial martial arts school. There is a teaching half, and an administrative half. Take my advice, you must pay equal attention to both halves if you want your school to grow.

In struggling schools, I typically see one person trying to keep up with everything. They're teaching the classes, answering the phones, enrolling the new students, selling the gear, and so on... geeeez! In the end, all areas of the business suffer because one person can only do so much. On the other hand, the most successful schools I network with have teams operating their businesses. They place a specialist in each key area of the school, beginning with the teaching and administrative halves. See if this makes sense to you...

Mostly all martial arts schools have one individual who is highest in the chain of command. This person is probably the owner. Usually, they are the best teacher, most talented fighter, and biggest martial arts fanatic in the school. From experience, I can tell you that these individuals typically make better instructors than they do businesspeople. It's best to let them stick to their strengths, and be Chief Instructors.

A Chief Instructor's job is to manage the teaching half of the school. This includes teaching the classes, developing the curriculum, creating testing procedures, building the Leadership Team, motivating the students, producing great black belts, serving as the school's leader, and more. This is an enormous responsibility that will ultimately determine the school's level of retention. And it doesn't matter how many students a school enrolls, if it can't keep the ones it has. Do the math. So managing the teaching half of the school is a full time job, and the Chief Instructor should treat it as such.

However, many instructors I consult with make teaching a part time job. That's because they're always bogged down with a zillion other duties that pull their focus away from the deck. So they end up working harder and harder for less results. What instructors like this could really use is a good Program Director to share the workload with.

Putting a competent Program Director in charge of the administrative half of a school can quickly decrease stress and increase productivity. While the Chief Instructor is on the deck, devoting one hundred percent effort to teaching great classes, the Program Director can be in the office focusing on administration. In fact, the Program Director will orchestrate the entire process of enrolling students from beginning to end. This includes handling information calls, teaching intros, conducting enrollment conferences, prospecting, following-up, renewing memberships, and more. Like the teaching half of the school, this half, too, is clearly a full-time job. Wouldn't you agree?

So why don't more struggling schools have Program Directors? Most claim that they can't seem to find the right person... year after year, after year. Yet, other schools have a waiting list for this position. That's odd. Could it be that certain instructors overcomplicate the search? Perhaps they don't truly understand what constitutes a good Program Director? In my experience, finding the right Program Director may not be as difficult as you think. Here are some tips.

Above all, I suggest scouting for someone who is exceptionally strong in two key areas. First, they should be a really good people-person. You want your Program Director to be charismatic, well spoken, and highly professional. Since it is the Program Director that will make the first impression on all new students entering your school, he/she must be a master of people skills... not necessarily of martial arts skills. That being the case, even a no-belt, spouse, or Leadership Team member could qualify if they receive proper training and have the right set of attributes.

Second, your Program Director should be an excellent salesperson. Think about it. They're selling when they teach introductory lessons, conduct enrollment conferences, answer information calls, present renewal agreements, etc. A powerful sidekick won't help them much in these areas. But strong consultative sales skills definitely will.

So the point is that there are two separate and completely distinct halves to operate within a commercial martial arts school. It's a mistake to try to run both halves alone. In my experience, this leads to a sloppy situation, poor results, and lots of unnecessary stress. There's simply too much to do, and not enough of any one person to go around. The solution, for many instructors, has been to find the right Program Director. This one employee can make all the difference in the world.

31: My Holy Trinity

A key staff member for martial arts schools is the Program Director. That was my main area of responsibility at John Graden's USA Karate in St. Petersburg, Florida. Based upon that experience, I can sum up the majority of my job description by mentioning just three critical activities—prospecting, presenting, and following-up.

Let's take a closer look at each of these three Key Result Areas (KRAs) one at a time.

1. Prospecting

As a Program Director, I always asked myself the question: "Where is my next student going to come from?" I quickly learned that the answer was through prospecting, which is the process of lead generation. This was the activity that ultimately led me to the results I was looking for—new students for our school. To that end, I spent at least 50% of my time prospecting.

Prospecting can occur in various ways. Low cost methods include flyers, door hangers, lead boxes, referral contests, buddy days, demonstrations, telemarketing, and so on. Then, of course, there are the more expensive methods, which include newspaper ads, auto-dial telemarketing machines, yellow page ads, television commercials, radio ads, etc. Personally, I suggest a combination of the two methods, to get your phone ringing and your door swinging. The key, however, is to be very active with your prospecting. Just making an occasional outbound telemarketing call, or having a monthly yellow page ad is rarely enough to pack your school with students. You've got to hit the market with a combination attack, at all times. That will create synergy with your prospecting efforts, and you'll begin to attract new student inquiries from many different sources instead of just a few.

2. Presenting

Presenting was my favorite part of the "trinity". It's the direct result of prospecting. Presenting occurs when you take prospective students on a tour of the school, conduct an introductory lesson, or host an enrollment or renewal conference. These are the pay dirt activities. So the more time your Program Director spends presenting the better. Typically, this activity accounted for about 15% of my time.

In section twenty-nine, we discussed the critical importance of Diagnostic Selling. As I mentioned, I've found that this process is the very best way to present students with the opportunity to join a martial arts school. That's why I strongly encourage you and your Program Director to master the art of Diagnostic Selling. It will make presenting your favorite part of the "trinity," too.

3. Following-up

Brian Tracy once said that a sales professional can increase his or her percentages for closing a sale by up to 1,000% simply by following-up. For a Program Director, no truer words have ever been spoken.

When I really focused on prospecting, leads began pouring in from all different directions. The last thing I wanted was for those valuable leads to go to waste. To put this in perspective, just think of how much each lead costs your school to acquire. For example, if you spend a thousand dollars on advertising and promoting during a particular month, and you receive ten leads, then each lead is worth one hundred dollars. Not following up on one of these leads is like burning a hundred-dollar bill. Following-up is mandatory, and you've got to pounce on your leads while they're hot. In fact, I suggest you follow-up on all leads within twenty-four hours. If you don't, then your leads will gradually go from hot, to warm, to cool, to cold.

Also, the more you prospect and present, the more following-up will be required. That's because prospective students often want to "think it over" or "talk to their other half" before joining. Don't let these people fade into the sunset. Following-up with prospects in this category is a must. Track them using a day-planner, computer, or hardcopy card system. Be persistent, but professional, and stay on 'em until you get a "yes" or "no" answer.

As a Program Director I wore many hats. My list of duties ranged from emptying the trash to teaching the blackbelt class. However, I never lost sight of the fact that my key result areas were prospecting, presenting, and following-up. This was my "holy trinity."

32: The Life Cycle of a Lead

I want to touch upon the sequence of events that allows a Program Director to transform an ordinary lead into a new student, and beyond. I call this sequence The Life Cycle of a Lead. I suggest that if you train your Program Director to become an autonomous expert at the following steps, you'll be able to substantially increase your growth, and focus much more on the teaching half of your school. That's why you got into this business in the first place... right?

1. Sets the Appointment
Let's say the lead's life cycle officially begins when a prospect calls your school. A competent Program Director will eagerly field that call before the third ring, ask all the right questions, build rapport, and quickly set an appointment to visit the school. A Program Director with excellent phone skills will be on and off the phone with an appointment set in just a few minutes flat.

2. Schedules the Intros
When the prospect arrives, (ensured by a confirmation call), they will fill out a guest information card, and receive a brief tour of the school. Then, it's off to the office where the Program Director will masterfully analyze the prospect's needs, review the benefits, and convey how martial arts training will help. If all goes well, the Program Director will successfully schedule the prospect to take an introductory course.

3. Teaches the Intros
Next, the Program Director confirms the intro lesson appointments, and teaches them. Here the Program Director's goal is to motivate more than educate, push emotional hot buttons, build rapport, and show the student (and/or their parents) that martial arts is a safe, fun, highly beneficial activity that they are fully capable of doing. From experience, I can tell you that two, fifteen to twenty minute benefit-oriented intros work well.

4. Conducts the Enrollment Conference
Once the intro lessons are complete, the Program Director must rosin up his bow, and orchestrate the enrollment conference. This is the pay dirt activity. All prior activities with the prospect from marketing on up were conducted so they could get to this important point. If the Program Director did a great job in the intro course, and if the overall school is razor sharp, then about 80% of the selling will have already been accomplished before the intro student ever enters the office. Still, an awesome Program Director should be a

master at selling just in case additional skills must be applied to help the prospective student make the right decision.

5. Helps the New Student Integrate

Handwritten notes, new student calls, emails, and office chats are effective in helping the new student feel at home. Most importantly though, I suggest that the Program Director assists in the white belt class. New students are like "fragile eggs," and the last thing the Program Director wants to do is initiate a relationship with the student, graduate them into the white belt class, and forget about them. No way. Instead, they should be out there on the deck (for at least a few minutes each class) to help the new student integrate into the school.

6. Seeks Referrals

During one of his/her new student phone calls, the Program Director asks for referrals. They should ask for as many as they can get. Referrals are the least expensive and highest quality leads your school will ever receive, and the best Program Directors use this to their advantage.

7. Conducts the Renewal Conference

With the Program Director's nurturing, the new student will make a smooth transition into the school. Going forward, the Program Director wants to make sure that he (and the rest of the staff) provides the highest levels of customer service possible. Why? Because soon it will be renewal time. A smart Program Director knows that if the customer service at his/her school is legendary, it will make their task of renewing students a whole lot easier.

By taking each student from a lead to a renewal, a Program Director absorbs much of the school's administrative workload. This allows the Chief Instructor to stay focused on teaching and building student retention. When it comes to growing a school, it's all about creating and keeping students. As The Life Cycle of a Lead illustrates, Program Directors are key to this process.

33: Five Ways to Compensate a Program Director

Looking for some fresh ideas on how to compensate a Program Director? The first step is to find out how much the prospective employee needs to earn. A dad with three kids and a wife has much different needs than a twenty-one year old bachelor. Second, find out how much they want to earn. In other words, what are their financial goals? Knowing these two important facts will help you determine if you can afford to hire the individual, and how to best structure their compensation plan so it's a win-win.

Here are five popular methods of compensation for you to consider.

1. The Volunteer Method

If you're just getting started, or simply can not afford to hire a salaried Program Director, then I suggest you look for a volunteer. A Leadership Team member, relative, student, or parent of one of your students could work. The idea is to have them help out on a short-term, part-time basis, while you develop enough cash flow to hire an employee to fill this critically important position.

2. The Commission Only Method

A risk free and affordable way to begin compensating a part-time Program Director is by paying them a commission for each enrollment they generate. In this case, you only end up paying for results, and you're actually paying for them with the revenue they create.

3. The Base Salary with Bonus Method

This method works well for a truly dedicated part-time or full-time Program Director. Provide them with an hourly wage that is fair based upon their talents, devotion, needs, and the average income in your area. This will comprise their base salary. Then, give them a bonus for each new student they enroll. Thirty to fifty dollars per enrollment is common.

4. The Enrollment Amount, Minus Base Salary Method

This method works great for compensating a full-time Program Director in an established school. Start by guaranteeing the employee a monthly base salary. Whatever the amount is, it should be enough to at least cover their monthly expenses. So, even if the school has a bad month, they will never earn less than their base. At month's end, multiply each of their new enrollments by a predetermined dollar amount. Then, subtract their base salary from their enrollment dollar amount to determine their bonus. Here's an

example: Let's say your Program Director's base salary is $2,000 per month, he accrues $100 for each new enrollment, and he enrolled thirty new students during a particular month. You would take their base salary of $2,000, and subtract it from an enrollment figure of $3,000. Using this example, the Program Director will walk away with a $1,000 bonus check on top of their base salary.

5. The Percentage Method

This method can become a bit complex. But the basic idea is to create a compensation plan that does not limit the Program Director's financial growth, yet gives the school the maximum amount of leverage when it comes to paying for performance. The first step is to determine how much of a salary you want to pay your Program Director after listening to their needs and wants. Next, assign a specific percentage to a combination of key areas relating to the school's current level of monthly performance that, when added up, equal the amount of salary you want to pay. These areas could include product sales, testing fees, collected tuition, contract amount written, etc. To make matters simple, some employers choose to base their Program Director's salary solely on a percentage of the total monthly gross. Either way, if the school slows or grows, the Program Director's salary adjusts proportionately. This method places a heavy emphasis on school-wide involvement and strong performance.

While there are certainly other methods for compensating Program Directors, these five are the most common. Keep in mind that they do not include health or dental insurance, 401K contributions, or paid vacation time, though you'll want to use extras such as these as negotiation tools. Go get 'em!

34: Make the Most of Your Marketing Dollar by Following Up

One of the least expensive and most effective ways to increase your enrollment is by making follow-up phone calls. These calls are critical for growth. As I mentioned earlier, studies have shown that following up on a missed sale increases your percentage of closure by 300 to 1,000 percent. Knowing this, can you really afford not to be making these calls?

The average martial arts school is constantly working to generate new leads. Demonstrations, lead boxes, distributing flyers, print advertising, school promotions, and referrals all provide valuable leads for gaining new students. For most instructors, getting fresh leads isn't the problem. However, following up on them is. This is a common weak spot, as many instructors let their valuable leads go to waste. That's no different than tearing up money.

Usually, follow-up calls are made by the school's Program Director. However, some schools are limited on staff, and must delegate this task to someone else. Just about anyone can make follow up calls as long as they are motivated, courteous, professional, and understand the benefits of martial arts training. Some schools even assign a well-trained member of their Leadership Team to this task. The key here is to properly prepare this individual through role-plays, and any other training tools you can get your hands on.

It's important to prioritize the tasks that will lead to a school's growth. Along these lines, telemarketing follow up calls have earned placement near the top of the list. Any new leads that are generated should be followed up on no later than 72 hours after initial contact with the prospect is made. Even better, a 24 hour call back policy is strongly recommended. The longer one delays following up, the less chance they have for acquiring a new student. It's important to be disciplined in this area, and follow up fast. In other words, you want to take a "get 'em while they're hot" attitude.

There are two main types of follow-up calls to consider:

Prospecting Follow-Up Call
The first is known as a "prospecting" follow-up call. Its main purpose is to set an appointment for a prospect to come in, tour the school, and watch a beginners' class. Typically, there is little to no selling during a prospecting follow-up call.

Sales Follow Up Call

The second type of follow-up call is known as a "sales" follow-up call. Its purpose is to get a "yes" or "no" answer out of a prospect who has already visited the school, or taken an introductory course. Here, the prospect may have deferred to higher authority, or said that they wanted to think it over. These potential students can be considered hot prospects, and 100% of them should receive a follow-up call on an agreed upon date and time. Don't let them slip away.

It's recommended that a minimum of 50-100 follow-up calls are made on a weekly basis. Just remember, the Law of Numbers directly applies to tele-marketing, so the more calls you make the better your results will be. Besides, much of the time and money you invest in lead generation simply goes to waste when leads are not followed up on promptly and effectively. Again, it's like tearing up money.

When telemarketing, efficiency is also an important skill. In fact, a good mar-tial arts telemarketer can usually be on and off the phone in about two to four minutes with an appointment set. How, you ask? Keep reading.

You'd be surprised how much time can be saved by not discussing the ori-gins of martial arts, the strengths and weaknesses of various styles, the cre-dentials of the school's owner, gossip about other local schools, payment arrangements, etc. Indeed, an expert on the phone will trim all of this fat, and get right to the heart of the matter.

Finally, each call and its details should be recorded. Details pertaining to the actual conversation should be listed in the prospect's file hardcopy or com-puter file. And all statistical data should be recorded on a stat sheet. A good telemarketing stat sheet would have categories for total amount of follow-up calls made, prospects contacted, appointments set, and prospects-contacted to appointment-set ratio. This will allow the person making the calls to keep track of their performance, and set goals. Ultimately, following-up will help you make the most of your marketing dollar.

Section Thirty-Four

35: How to Select a Tuition Billing Company

One of the most common questions our NAPMA consultants receive is, "Which billing company should I choose to handle my school's tuition?" Since this question has always been so common, I'd like to provide a response.

First of all, it's important to realize that it's very difficult for a consultant to decide what billing company is best for you. That's because selecting the right billing company depends heavily on your personal situation, and therefore it involves a lot of research. Don't forget, the billing company you choose will handle the vast majority of your school's revenue, and will often deal directly with your students. That's pretty serious. So it's not the kind of decision that I would recommend leaving up to someone else's discretion. Instead, I suggest the following:

Step 1: Research the Market
The first step to take when selecting a tuition billing company is to research the market. You want to investigate as many companies as possible. That way you can get a feel for what's out there, and begin narrowing down your options. Just a friendly word of advice: do your homework before you make a final decision.

Step 2: Contact Them by Phone
After you've narrowed down the companies you're interested in, make a list of the questions you want answered. Then, call each of them for information. Ask them to explain why you should choose them over one of their competitors. Let them do their best to sell you on their service. If they truly care about your business, they'll work very hard to gain it.

Step 3: Have Them Mail You Information
After the billing company representative has answered all of your questions, ask them to send you some information for further evaluation. Be up-front, and tell them that you're shopping around because you want to make the best decision for your school.

Once you receive their information packet, it's very important to read it over carefully. You want to read all the fine print, and check into every possible detail. For example, you'll want to find out if there are any additional fees, such as annual membership dues, special NSF collection charges, account cancellation fees, monthly minimums, etc. What percentage of collections do they get, and how does this compare to their competitors? How many times do they redraft NSF accounts, and when? What is their policy if you want to switch billing companies? Must you use their service exclusively? How does this company actually make its money, when their ads say they charge so little? These are the kinds of questions I suggest you find out before finally selecting a billing company.

Step 4: Speak to Some of Their Clients
In my opinion, talking to a billing company's clients is one of the best ways to get an accurate description of their service. Of course, the company's salespeople will tell you their service is the best in the field. Yeah, yeah… what I want to know is what their clients think of them.

I recommend getting the names and numbers of at least five of their clients. Also, I suggest getting this information from a source other than the billing company, if possible. Why? Because you can guarantee that if they select the names, they're going to pick their friends, most satisfied clients, and the individuals they know will give their company the best review. That's natural. Personally, I prefer non-biased testimonials.

Step 5: Make a Decision
Once you've researched the market, spoken to the different companies' representatives, reviewed their information, and gotten a real world description of their track record, it's time to make an educated decision. After all of that is said and done, you'll have a good conscience knowing that you made every effort to select the best company to handle your school's billing.

Finally, I'd like to say that at NAPMA, we recommend that schools use a tuition billing company just as long as it makes sense based upon each individual's unique set of circumstances. We believe that it can be confusing to students if a school owner is both the "good sensei" and "evil bill-collector" at the same time. Plus, we instructors are typically "softies" when it comes to our students. That can get expensive.

Even more, it can be counterproductive from a time management standpoint for an owner to be in the office making collection calls, instead of on the deck teaching. And who needs the headaches? So delegating this service out to a company that specializes in it is key. The trick is finding the right one for you. Good luck!

36: How to Start Keeping Statistics

If you're an instructor that does not keep statistics, but would like to start, here's how I suggest you begin.

The first step is to make keeping statistics a habit. You've got to make it a habit, just like brushing your teeth in the morning. In fact, I suggest that you never shut your school down for the evening until you've tallied that day's numbers. That requires a lot of self-discipline. But you already have plenty of that, right?

The next step is to get yourself a nice three-ring binder. This will serve as your stat book. Then, you'll want to create and include a simple control form that allows you to track the following basic statistics:

Information Calls
Keep a pad and pen near every phone in your school. Whenever someone calls to inquire about classes, put a tick mark in the blank for that day. Also, track how they heard about you, so you know where to best invest your marketing dollars. At the end of each day, transfer the total number of calls, and how they heard about you, to your stat book.

Appointments Set
Whenever you receive a qualified information call, the goal is to schedule that person for an appointment to visit your school. Be sure to record the total number of daily appointments set in your stat book. This will enable you to determine an information-call to appointment-set ratio, which will help you gauge the effectiveness of your phone skills.

Introductory Lessons
Each day, record the amount of first and second lesson intros you taught. This is important information. If your stats show a pattern of students not completing their introductory course, then you know you have to adjust your introductory material or approach.

Enrollments
Of course, you'll need to keep track of your glorious enrollments. If this number does not equal at least 80% of your completed introductory lessons, you have some work to do. You'll have to determine why people are not enrolling more often. It could be price, quality, schedule, competition, your presentation skills, etc. Whatever the objections are, you must figure out a way to overcome them.

Collected Revenue

In most schools, revenue is generated from tuition, down payments, product sales, and special events. You want a separate category on your stat sheet for each source of revenue you have. Using subcategories is also recommended. For example, under tuition you may create a subcategory for EFTs, credit cards, down payments, cash, etc. Each day, add up the amounts to determine your total collected revenue.

Active Student Count

There are lots of ways to determine your active count. Perhaps the easiest is to count all the students who attended class at least twice this month, and consider them active. Others consider a student inactive once they miss three or more weeks of training. It's really up to you.

While there are many other statistics you could keep, these represent the basics. Once you have them on paper, the next step is to learn how to analyze them to your advantage. For example, if you received fifteen information calls, but only scheduled five appointments, you know that you have to brush up your telephone skills. Or, if you taught ten introductory lessons, and only enrolled three students, then you know your enrollment conference needs work. Get the idea?

One of the fastest ways to begin keeping track of your statistics, if you do not already have a system in place, is to implement NAPMA's Financial Control and Retention System. This very basic, yet powerful series of forms for retention and statistical control is included in NAPMA's new member start-up kit. As long as you are a NAPMA member, you can always contact us to receive an additional copy for free.

Knowing your numbers allows you to create an action plan for improving the results in every area of your school. If you do not have this information at your fingertips, you're flying blind. Not to mention you might get ninja'd by Uncle Sam, as was the case with a school owner I spoke with recently.

Finally, keep in mind that if you don't know where you've been, it's hard to know where you are going. Keeping accurate statistics will give you direction, and enable you to set goals. As an owner or operator of a martial arts school, few things are more important.

37: Be Careful with Paid-in-Full Memberships

Every so often a new buzz works its way through the martial arts industry. So what's the latest buzz? Well, it has to due with paid-in-full memberships (PIFs), otherwise known as cash-outs. Let me help you understand why people are suddenly talking about this subject.

Cash-outs are nothing new. However, recently there seems to be a strong movement towards high numbers of high dollar cash-outs in schools across the country. By now you've probably heard the lavish success stories of instructors grossing large amounts of money month after month. I'm talking about $50K, $60K, $70K in single month! How, you ask? I'm told it's because these instructors are collecting most of their students' tuition dollars up front, and before their students have a chance to drop out.

Some instructors are applying this "get as much money, as quickly as possible" strategy to all age groups of students, as often as they can, and without batting an eyelash. The reason for this is obvious. Instructors can make a whole lot more money much quicker. One concern, though, is that retention can become an afterthought in a situation where most students have already paid for years of lessons in advance, and paid the maximum they could possibly afford. I'm certainly not implying that all instructors who conduct a high volume of cash-outs stop focusing on student retention, but the reality is that some instructors are likely to give in to the temptation. We must be careful here.

Recently, a variety of well-known industry leaders and instructors have voiced their concerns. For starters, EFC Chairman Nick Cokinos vigorously comments, "Martial arts schools are facing a serious decision. Are we a selling organization, or a service organization? A selling organization is pretty clearly defined in that there is a crew of salesmen out there maximizing the sale of their product. A service organization is radically different, in that it is an academy, oriented around student service, and totally involved in a close student-teacher relationship designed to bring out the best in each and every one of its students. That's the top priority, not how much money you can get out of them before they quit."

Likewise, other industry heavyweights have expressed integrity-based apprehensions. The President of IFC/EasyPay, Rick Bell, points out, "Now that our industry is finally experiencing some mainstream acceptance as a valid education form, we would do well to demonstrate some restraint when it comes to extracting money from a trusting student. Just because we can do a thing, does not mean that we should do a thing. Should instructors use their power and position to talk the parents of a five year old into paying them cash in advance for a multi-year program?"

While these concerns are valid, cash-outs certainly aren't a bad thing when used correctly. One of the first leaders to widely educate our industry on the proper use of cash-outs was NAPMA founder John Graden, in his best-selling book *How to Open and Operate a Successful Martial Arts School*. Here, Graden teaches, "PIFs are dangerous to the degree that you:

1. Spend the money before you've earned it. I recommend you open a special reserve account for PIF revenue, and let it build to offset the liability of the lessons you owe. Your liability account should never drop below the amount of outstanding lessons you still owe.

2. Have inconsistencies in your enrollments. If you have months when you enroll twenty people, followed by months of enrolling just five, then you cannot rely on PIFs. Obviously, in the months you enroll just five people, your income is going to take a huge hit. Your other PIF students are no longer sources of real income. You are totally dependent on new PIFs coming in, and if they do not, you end up scrambling to meet your obligations."

As you can see, instructors must use cash-outs intelligently because there are numerous risk factors involved. In the past, many professionals in our field have proven that they are better athletes than money-managers… hence the need for billing companies. Instead of putting cash-out money into a reserve account, as John Graden recommends, instructors typically spend it. This can lead to devastating consequences in the wake of a market downturn, a competition-related slowdown, lawsuits, refund requests, or an injury that prevents the main instructor from teaching. Plus, how much is a school worth to a potential buyer when all the students are cashed-out, and there is no money in the bank? The answer is: not much. Folks, these risks are real, and they must be taken seriously.

As past history has taught us, the road to cash-outs can be laced with many land mines if one does not handle them correctly. Again, I'm not saying that cash-outs are bad. Actually, they can be very positive if you use them to supplement your regular monthly tuition collections. However, I do think cash-outs should be used in moderation and with the right blend of ethics, moral practice, and integrity. After all, we are martial artists.

38: How to Conduct a Successful Staff Meeting

Several times each week, the in-house NAPMA staff automatically makes their way to the conference room for our general staff meetings. With the scent of fresh brewed coffee dancing in the air, they eagerly seat themselves around the mahogany conference table. A variety of Day Planners, Palm Pilots, and legal pads are open like steel traps as the team prepares to map out their day.

With so many important projects in the works, and a diverse staff of professionals, I depend heavily on these meetings to keep the association running smoothly. They help the entire NAPMA team to improve customer service, get motivated, stay organized, communicate with one another, prioritize activities, meet deadlines, create goals, enhance performance, and come up with lots of new exciting ideas. As you can imagine, these daily meetings are absolutely critical to our success.

After hosting our meetings for many years now, I've discovered a number of ways to make them as efficient and productive as possible. Now I'd like to share some of those tips with you, so that you can make your staff meetings the best that they can possibly be.

Write Down Meeting Topics
Creating the content for a meeting is easy if you work on it little by little throughout the day. In other words, whenever something comes up that you'd like to discuss in a future staff meeting, immediately write it down. A standard Daytimer can be used for this. Each day, open it to the date of your next meeting, and start a list under the heading Today's Meeting. By doing this, you'll never forget your ideas and employee observations.

Distribute an Outline
Before the start of any meeting, provide each staff member with an outline of the topics about to be discussed. This handout will give the meeting direction, and keep it moving at a steady pace. Most importantly, it will prevent you from wasting time, or getting off-track. Remember, always go into your meetings knowing ahead of time what you want to discuss.

Assign a Minute-Taker
A minute-taker is someone who records the details of a meeting as they are discussed. After the meeting, that person then types out a clean version of the minutes, and provides each staff member with a copy. This is important as it helps remind everyone of their new assignments, and exactly what was covered in the meeting.

Follow-Up

During each staff meeting, allocate a few moments to review the minutes that were taken in the previous meeting. This will give you an opportunity to follow-up on assigned projects. As you know, some staff members may procrastinate, or forget their assignments. Following-up will prevent this from happening.

Be Motivational

One of the main purposes of a staff meeting is to motivate the staff. You want to psych-them-up, if you will. When this is done successfully, your team will leave the meeting feeling great about themselves, and eager to get back to work. If they leave feeling deflated, disappointed, or upset, then you did something wrong. Always end your meetings on a positive note.

Keep the Meetings Professional

During a staff meeting, it's important to keep the level of professionalism high. For example, teach your staff not to interrupt other staff members before they're finished speaking. They should learn to respect each other's opinions and ideas. Likewise, they should know not to use profanity, or crack jokes every two seconds. This can become very distracting. When simple guidelines such as these are followed, you'll get a lot more accomplished in your meetings.

Make Staff Meetings Mandatory

In my opinion, staff meetings should not be optional. They should be mandatory. In fact, I recommend building staff meetings directly into your employees' work hours. So the staff actually gets paid to attend them. In this situation, missing a meeting is just like missing work. Using this strategy, you should get 100% attendance and participation at every single meeting.

Always Keep a Positive Attitude

It's important that, as the host of the meeting, you do your best to keep a positive attitude. Like all good leaders, you too must try to become an unshakable optimist. Avoid letting your staff see you upset, angry, or stressed-out when things aren't going according to plan. Even though this may be difficult, the fact is that you must sometimes mask your emotions for the good of the group.

Finally, I want to point out that my first rule of thumb where meetings are concerned is to avoid them if possible. That's right! Meetings cost you time and money. I'd rather have my team producing, instead of sitting in the conference room with a cup of coffee talking about producing. However, meetings are indeed necessary and valuable. But they must be handled properly. So, from now on, when you host your staff meetings, be sure to employ the universal tips mentioned above, to make them run smoother, and more efficiently.

39: The "Big-Three" Meetings and Their Content

In the last passage, I provided you with a variety of practical ideas for hosting a more efficient staff meeting. Now that the stage has been set, I'd like to take this discussion to the next level. I'm going to describe for you three types of meetings that can be used to improve your staff's performance—guaranteed!

1. Monday Morning Meeting

The most important meeting of the week is the one held on Monday morning. It is here where you review the previous week's details, and preview the week to come. This meeting typically lasts for at least one hour, and should be heavily focused on retention-building strategies.

In fact, I suggest that you begin every Monday meeting with the A, B, C rating system. This is when the staff reviews an alphabetical list of every single student in the school and collectively rates them A, B, or C based upon attitude, level of participation and performance. If done consistently, the A, B, C rating system will positively impact your retention.

The first meeting of the week is also an excellent time to pass out weekly goal commitment sheets. These sheets will help each staff member to organize their priorities for the week, and set individual standards of performance. Ideally, this should keep them focused on key areas of importance throughout the week.

In addition, the Monday meeting is perfect for discussing any strides the staff has made in the area of self-education. But in order to make this part of your Monday meetings you must first create a continuance of education program for your staff.

The best way to launch a staff education program is to build a powerful collection of books, videos, and audio materials for them to use. Just like at the public library, staff members can check materials out, but must return them when they're finished. A program like this will keep their knowledge growing in key areas such as customer service, sales, motivation, psychology, charisma, leadership, business, martial arts history, and more. The whole idea is to help them become better at their profession.

Once such a program is in place, you can give your staff a weekly continuing education form to fill out, and bring back to every Monday meeting. Then, each staff member would have a few moments to share their new information with the group. This is a great way for your staff members to learn from one another as well.

2. Daily Meeting
Your staff should also get in the habit of having a daily meeting. This brief meeting lasts about 15 minutes, and occurs shortly before students and parents begin arriving at the school.

Daily meetings are extremely helpful since they help coordinate the staff's efforts for that day. Topics such as the day's appointments, retail deliveries, lesson plans, test preparation, and renewals are commonly discussed. These meetings are particularly advantageous in schools that have several staff members, such as a Receptionist, a Chief Instructor, a Program Director, Assistant Instructors, etc.

3. Friday Meeting
Friday meetings also last for about an hour, but are different from Monday meetings in a number of ways. Mainly, they're a lot more laid back, and are often used for staff training. In fact, Fridays are great for making curriculum adjustments, brainstorming, or developing professional skills.

Role playing, for example, is a typical Friday meeting activity. Here, staff members pair-off, and practice vital skills such as setting appointments over the phone, overcoming objections, teaching introductory lessons, renewing students, and dealing with upset parents. This kind of training will help the staff to stay sharp, and maintain their professional skills.

Also, I recommend injecting some excitement into your Friday meetings by hosting them away from your school. You might consider meeting at a restaurant over breakfast or lunch. This kind of environment presents a great opportunity for brainstorming. Another idea is to take turns gathering at different staff members' houses. Of course, the current week's host would provide refreshments like coffee, juice, fruits, bagels, etc. In this case, it's convenient for the team to watch an educational video such as the kind that NAPMA provides every month. After the video, the staff can compare notes, and discuss how the information can be applied to your school.

By hosting these types of meetings regularly, and with the correct substance, you will be able to groom your instructors into expert teachers, efficient time managers, dedicated sales professionals, and charismatic leaders. Even more, you will increase communication, and eliminate confusion. But best of all, you'll put your school on the fast track to success!

40: Do You Over-Deliver on Customer Service?

When you chose martial arts as your profession, you chose to work in the service industry. That means that you are a servant to your students. It's not the other way around. And since we live and die by the quality of the service we provide, that service had better be legendary.

My rule of thumb is to always give clients more than they expect. Promise high, and then over-deliver. But before you can do this, you have to believe in your heart that your customers deserve the very best service you can possibly give. We're in the twenty-first century, and 100% is the minimum your students deserve. In my opinion, that's what you provide if you only want to survive. If you really want to plow past your competition and flourish, then give your customers 110% in everything you do. Again, over-deliver.

Let's face it, most businesses do not follow this policy. Indifferent, underpaid, detached, robotic, employees often make us feel like they're doing us a favor for allowing us to spend our money there. Indeed, they've got it backwards. Recently, a waiter spilled a drink on a friend of mine, and expected him to pay for half of it. Yeah, that's great service. The kind that can put a For Rent sign in your front window. And next time some kid wearing a barbell in his tongue doesn't say thank you after I pay him, I'm gonna smack him over the head with this book. The list of bad customer service examples I could give is endless, but you get the idea.

In fact, mediocre customer service seems to be the norm. As a society, we've gotten numb to it. That's why it shouldn't be difficult for your martial arts school to stand out amongst the crowd. If you really want to blow your customers away, just give them better service than they are use to getting everywhere else. Your clients will rave about you, and your retention will soar. That's exactly what we experience at NAPMA. We constantly over-deliver.

Sadly though, the quality of the service in a lot of martial arts schools is just as bad as the service everywhere else. It's no wonder that the majority of schools stay small. It's typically not because their martial arts skills are weak, it's because the overall service they provide is poor.

Many schools need a complete customer service overhaul spanning from how they answer their phone to what they teach as their curriculum. These service-oriented weak spots commonly include—general follow-up skills, professional billing procedures, leadership skills, school cleanliness, over-inflated egos, quality and quantity of staff members, program variety, convenient scheduling, and group presentation skills. Any of these flaws can prevent a school from growing. Hmm, isn't it interesting that the average school only has about 150 students?

In my experience, most schools that suffer from poor customer service policies do so because of the leadership at the top. It's the owners that hold their schools back the most. For example, certain instructors fight to maintain the non-customer-service-oriented, old school ways they came up with. Other instructors don't know what good customer service is, due to their background. And others simply don't care to improve upon their customer service because their school exists to serve themselves, not their customers.

The bottom line is that you must give outstanding customer service if you expect to achieve high levels of success. You've got to be willing to bend over backwards for your students, and treat them like gold. And you must teach your staff to do the same. This requires policies, procedures, and lots of practice.

Look at it this way. Your students pay your salary, your rent, and your instructors' salaries. Without them, you'd have no more school. That being the case, wouldn't you say it's important to over-deliver on customer service?

41: Do Your Students Realize How Much You Care?

You've heard the old saying, "Little things mean alot." Well, that saying holds especially true when trying to retain students in a martial arts school.

If you appreciate your students, you've got to let them know it. Otherwise, they may feel like they're just one of the herd. When this happens, it becomes easy for them to stray away from your school, and get involved in other activities.

Instead, I recommend that you make every student in your school feel special as often as possible. When students feel like they're important, and believe that you have a genuine interest in them, they become emotionally attached to your program. They begin to look upon you as a special friend rather than just a paid martial arts instructor. Building a relationship like this with your students takes a lot of effort, but it can have a huge impact on your retention. Guaranteed!

One way that you can show students how you care is by mailing them a variety of cards. The cards must be hand-written, and specifically tailored to the recipient! Do not use cards that have a machine-stamped message inside. They are terribly impersonal, and lack substance. Also, it is important to place an actual stamp on the envelope, and hand-write the address information. Running the envelopes through a postage meter, or using computer-generated labels, takes away any sense of personalization, and will give your card a junk-mail appearance.

Here are five types of cards that any school can begin mailing to make their students feel more appreciated:

1. Praise Cards: It's a good idea to get the entire staff in the habit of mailing out at least two "praise" or "good job" cards, per day, to your students. The message written on the inside should praise your students for something they've done. It could be for outstanding attendance, assisting in class, curriculum improvements, academic excellence, technical skills, etc. When a student does something commendable, don't keep it a secret. Drop them a note in the mail, or highlight them in front of the class. That will show them that what they've done hasn't gone unnoticed. Also, it will encourage them to keep up the good work.

2. Welcome-Aboard Cards: Every new student who joins your school should receive a welcome-aboard card within 48 hours after their enrollment. Sending these cards is a critical step in the enrollment process. Again, they should be hand-written, and personalized by your Program Director, or who-ever enrolls new students into your school.

Also, these cards can mitigate buyer's remorse. In other words, they can help remove any doubt a new student might have about their decision to join your school. So, if you really want to help your new students validate their enroll-ment decision, make sure you send them a welcome-aboard card... pronto.

3. Attendance Cards: Sending out "We Miss You" or "Class Just Isn't the Same Without You" cards is super important. Of course, calling students on the phone to find out where they've been, is the best approach. But, mailing them a card with a hand-written message is an excellent back-up. When students receive your card, they'll realize that you actually noticed that they haven't been in class. This shows them you're concerned, and makes them feel important. Whether you create your own cards, or buy them directly, make sure that the Chief Instructor at your school sends these cards out regularly.

4. Birthday Cards: You may also consider mailing out birthday cards to your students. They should already be getting cards from family members and close friends around this time. Sending them a birthday card, too, will help your students associate their "karate school family" with the other people who care about them the most.

By investing in a good martial arts software for your school's computer, you can easily keep track of each student's date of birth. This will enable you to quickly generate a list of birthdays every month. Then, you can invest in a vari-ety of inexpensive birthday cards, such as the kind that NAPMA offers, and mail them out at the beginning of each new month. This is a nice gesture that will really make students feel special. They won't believe that you remembered!

5. Appointment Cards: Here's another great idea. Anytime you book a new appointment, send them a "We're Looking Forward to Meeting You!" post-card with a short hand-written note. This is so simple, and easy to do. You'll be amazed at how much it will decrease your percentage of no-shows, and enlighten your appointments as to how professional your school is, before they ever even walk through the front door.

42: How to Transform Students into Staff with a Leadership Team

I n my opinion, staff building is the limiting factor in the growth and development of most martial arts schools. Let's face it, it can be challenging to build a staff given the field we're in.

After all, only about 1% of the population practices martial arts to begin with. Out of that 1%, at least 60% of our student population is comprised of children. Obviously, kids do not qualify as prospective staff members until they grow up. So, that narrows the selection pool down even further. Out of the prospects we have left, how many of them actually want to become professional martial artists like us? How many of them already have careers? How many of these prospects can actually afford to work at a martial arts school, given the financial arrangements and bare-bones benefit packages that are typically offered?

The fact is that most schools have tiny budgets, especially in the early stages of their development. While there are plenty of schools out there that do indeed generate a substantial income, and can afford to hire a staff, the majority of schools I consult with can't. It's simply not in their budget. So, it's a catch twenty-two. They know they need a staff in order to grow, but they don't have the money to pay one. So, the question many staff-less instructors would like answered is: How do they develop a staff, considering their limited budget? How do they get one started? Here's the answer.

The first step many successful schools took towards building their staff, was to develop a Leadership Team. In fact, when I chat with top instructors, I often ask them the following question:"Knowing what you now know about operating a successful commercial martial arts school, if you had to start all over again, what are some of the main things you would do to climb back up to the top of the heap?" Almost always, within their first few responses, they say, "I would develop a Leadership Team." That's why I recommend that you do the same.

You see, Leadership Team is the foundation for future staff at your school. It's your bench strength, and you can start one no matter how big or small your school may be. Ultimately, it's your best shot at transforming students into staff members over the course of time. And, for the most part, it's free to you.

The way staff building stems from a Leadership Team is simple. Your Leadership Team members begin assisting in class, often as adolescent under-ranks. Over time, they become leaders in your school, young adults, and black belts. Eventually, these people will need jobs, and many of them would love to do what you do for a living. Plus, they've already had a small taste of the gratification that goes along with being a martial arts instructor, just from participating on your Leadership Team. This is the perfect opportunity for you to offer them jobs as paid Assistant Instructors. From there, you'll have a good shot at developing them into salaried Chief Instructors, Program Directors, Managers of branch locations, etc.

What's interesting is that many schools have a surplus of staff members, using this method. That was certainly the case at the school where I did all my training. We had more staff members than we knew what to do with. Furthermore, whenever a staff member left our school, an ambitious Leadership Team member immediately replaced them. But the only reason we had this situation was because we had a strong Leadership Team program.

Now, let me change gears for just a moment. It's important to realize that the goal behind effective management is to get your work done through the help of other people. That requires a staff. You can't do it all by yourself forever. You're going to need some assistance. That's how any business grows beyond the limits of how far one person can take it. Therefore, if you plan to grow a commercial martial arts school, one of your key result areas (KRAs) should be team-building. How do you plan to build your staff? What's your strategy? Do you have one in place? If not, the odds of you building a staff are slim.

In conclusion, I think it's important to reaffirm that building a staff at a martial arts school takes creativity, continuous scouting, and proper planning. For most school owners, there's no quick and easy way to find employees. Unlike other small businesses, we can't just run an ad in the newspaper, and expect to be flooded with calls. Instead, we have to take a different approach. We have to be prepared to take a long-term perspective on staff development. So, unless you have unlimited resources, a Leadership Team could be the best way for you to build your staff.

43: How to Structure Your Leadership Team for Success

As we've already discussed, creating a solid Leadership Team can help you build the staff of your dreams. Now, I'd like to give you some pointers that will enable you to structure a successful Leadership Team program in your school, immediately.

Let me start by saying that a properly structured Leadership Team program is a win-win situation. Think of it this way. People come to your school to learn self-defense, get in shape, become a black belt, etc. And they receive all of these benefits, but, when they join your Leadership Team, they get so much more.

First, Leadership Team members learn how to overcome the number one fear: public speaking. Second, they learn how to teach. As you know, one of the best ways for students to fully understand their techniques, is to learn how to teach them to others. Third, Leadership Team members are taught how to be leaders within your school. That's an invaluable skill that will benefit them for the rest of their lives.

Likewise, Leadership Team offers a variety of benefits to your school. Your team members can assist you with warm ups, cool downs, and stretching. They are taught to keep a close eye out for safety while you're teaching. In addition, Leadership Team members can be trained to assist with attendance procedures, make new students feel welcome, help students who are struggling with their material during class, and coach small groups on basic material. Essentially, Leadership Team members allow you (the Chief Instructor) to become a multiplication sign. This is extremely helpful, especially if your school has a small staff. And, as we discussed last month, Leadership Team is your foundation for future staff. That's the biggest benefit of all for instructors.

When it comes to selecting Leadership Team members, I suggest you select based upon attitude, first. Students who rarely miss a class, support your school 100%, have strong social skills, and enjoy helping others always work best. The quality of their technique is important, but it's secondary. Imagine the opposite of this. Your best fighter joins your Leadership Team. He's not very sociable, and doesn't enjoy working with others. Let's just say he isn't going to make a very good Leadership Team member. That's why it's recommended that you nominate based upon attitude, primarily.

Once you select your Leadership Team members, you must create a Leadership Team class with a well-structured curriculum. This is the main focus of NAPMA's Guidance on Leadership Development (GOLD) program. Our goal with this program is to give you the monthly lesson plans and top quality material you need to transform students into leaders, and give them true value when they become part of your Leadership Team.

During Leadership Team class, it's common to practice drills that teach your members how to teach properly, how to ensure safety in the classroom, how to identify and assist "C" students, how to motivate, how to be an effective communicator, how to conduct mini-private lessons, etc. If you're going to have a Leadership Team program, you must have some kind of a Leadership Team class. Otherwise, you're gypping your students.

Next, I recommend you appoint a Leadership Team Captain. The strategy is to let the captain be in charge of your team, so you can focus on other activities that only you can do for your school. His or her duties would commonly include; scheduling team members to help out in your daily classes, monitoring the performance of each team member, developing the team's leadership skills, documenting team activities for your school's protection, following up, organizing team events, and providing you with detailed reports. For an owner, appointing a Leadership Team Captain is an example of smart management, good teamwork, and effective delegation.

Now, I think it's important to point out what Leadership Team is not. It's definitely not a way for you to get free help, so you can avoid hiring a paid staff. If your Leadership Team members become free workers, then you'll run the risk of opening yourself up to various labor law violations. Furthermore, Leadership Team members should not teach classes in place of the Chief Instructor. That's your job. Their job is to assist with classes, and be role models to the other students. There's a big difference. Just be careful not to take advantage of your team.

Finally, I'd like to mention that it's risky to waive or reduce a Leadership Team member's normal class fee in trade for assisting, since the IRS considers bartering to be a taxable event. While the odds of the government catching up with you for this are probably remote, it's best to play by the rules. For this reason, it's recommended that you continue to charge your team members at least their regular tuition. In fact, some Leadership Team programs are so comprehensive that owners charge thousands of extra dollars for students to participate. If the value is there, students will pay for it.

If you haven't started your Leadership Team yet, I suggest you do. From experience, I can tell you that it can be very rewarding. But, please, realize that before you can teach others how to be a leader, you must first be a good leader yourself. That takes constant effort. So, study hard, practice what you preach, and always lead by example.

44: Create a System for Feedback Within Your School

As martial arts professionals, it's important to realize that we're in a service business. We work with humans, and that requires high levels of customer service in order to be successful. When you get right down to it, this means giving students 110% service… 100% of the time.

But, in order to achieve this, you must first know exactly how your students and parents perceive your current level of customer service. Therefore, it's important to determine what good customer service means to them, not you. Indeed, the best way to accomplish this is to create a system for acquiring feedback on a regular basis. To help you get started, here are five suggestions that you can immediately use as part of your feedback system:

1. Office Chats

Office chats are spontaneous meetings with students that occur during normal business hours, and last for just a few minutes each. These little talks are excellent for motivating "C" students, following-up, or just making general conversation.

Since office chats present such a terrific opportunity for giving and receiving feedback, I recommend that each staff member at your school conduct at least two per day.

2. The Golden Suggestion Box

The golden suggestion box is a subtle and on-going way to acquire feedback from both students and parents. Here's how it works. Simply get a cardboard box, cut a rectangular slot in the top, and gift wrap it with some shiny gold paper. Then, put the box in a private part of the school.

Mention to your students that the box is gold because "their comments and suggestions are worth their weight in gold to you." Whenever someone feels the need to tell you what's on their mind, they can anonymously drop their comments in the box.

3. Tele-Feedback

Tele-feedback occurs over the phone, and can be extremely valuable when it comes to improving customer service. In fact, some of the best tele-feedback you can get is by conducting verbal exit surveys. Here, your goal is to find out exactly why students have stopped their training. Keep track of all comments, look for a pattern, and make your adjustments accordingly. This is extremely important!

Another excellent way to get tele-feedback is by making "New Student" calls. Several of these calls are typically made in the first six weeks of a new student's training; hence the name. They're great for "just checking in", detecting potential challenges, or asking for referrals. By now you've probably heard of these calls. The question is... are you doing them?

4. Written Surveys
One of the quickest ways to find out how your students feel about your school is to administer written surveys. Also, since written surveys are anonymous, they are particularly effective in finding out what students and parents really think about the overall quality of your school.

Verbal feedback sometimes gets sugar-coated because students are often intimidated by their instructors. Too, they may hold back to avoid hurting anyone's feelings. But since written surveys are anonymous, students and parents have the opportunity to be brutally honest. As painful as it may be, that's exactly what you want. I recommend distributing written surveys on a quarterly basis.

5. Feedback Forums
It's also beneficial to host a forum once or twice a year, to gain additional feedback from your adult students and the parents of your junior students.

In the forum, you would simply discuss important topics relevant to the betterment of the school. The key is to be prepared, and make sure that everyone leaves feeling like their opinion matters. Instill in them that your school is a democracy, and that you're counting on their feedback to make the school a better place for everyone involved. In fact, you can further this notion by publishing the important results of the forum in your newsletter.

By creating a system for acquiring feedback, top-level schools across the nation have successfully opened the communication lines between students and staff. This has enabled them to dramatically improve the quality of their customer service, and ultimately boost retention.

Many of these schools currently use the five methods for obtaining feedback mentioned above. So we already know that they work. Best of all these tips are easy to implement, and cost practically nothing to do. You never know... you may even have some shiny gold wrapping paper left over from the last holiday season.

45: Why Your Best Staff Members Might Leave You

In business, your most valuable resource is the human resource. This is especially true at a martial arts school because we operate in such a niche industry. Employees can be difficult to find, and top-notch ones even harder. When you do find a truly exceptional employee, it's important that you make every effort to keep them. They're like gold. Don't be short sighted in this area, or you'll end up losing your best people in the long run. Here are three common mistakes to watch out for with the people who contribute the most to you.

1. Lack of Recognition
Always recognize a job well done. If you do not give your key people the recognition they deserve, it could lead to low morale, a gradual decline in their performance, and eventual resentment. After being in the trenches all day, every day, top producers expect credit to be given where credit is due. They want to be praised, noticed, listened to, and treated with respect. They want to feel appreciated. According to Jeff Frick, President of Murria and Frick Insurance, "Good employees will leave if they perceive their talents and strengths aren't being acknowledged." Arguably, this single factor is responsible for more good employees quitting jobs than any other reason, including sensitive monetary issues.

2. Lack of Opportunity
Quality of life is a concern for most everyone in today's work force, especially among go-getters. If your best staff members no longer feel your school will help them meet their life goals, and you do not sweeten the pot, then they will be much more apt to consider other employment opportunities when and if they come along. Battle of Atlanta founder, Joe Corley comments, "Always try to provide the fairest, most professional, nurturing, and caring environment you can, and truly seek to provide great personal growth and financial opportunities for your key people."

To boost staff retention, some owners think long-term, and create bonus plans that allow their best employees to grow along with the school. Others provide investment opportunities such as stock options, limited partnerships, or actual ownership positions through franchising. Increased wages and promotions are also great morale boosters. In general, incentives such as these can keep key employees happy, committed, and locked in. But this can only be possible if the school owner is willing to go the extra mile for his/her best people.

3. Lack of Compensation
Another common exit factor among top producing staff members is not enough money or benefits to satisfy their needs and wants. Sometimes this occurs because the school genuinely can't afford certain employees—they're over-qualified, or they need too much to make ends meet. Other times, it's because of overly frugal owners being penny-wise and dollar-foolish. IFC

President Rick Bell adds, "My best advice for owners who want to keep good employees is to SHARE THE WEALTH. If you ignore the market, and pay them far less than they could earn on their own, they will soon figure out the game, and be gone. Remember that the employees who are most valuable to you will also be very, very valuable to themselves."

Now, here's the kicker! In the martial arts business, there are virtually no barriers to entry. So it's very easy for an instructor to leave your school, and start a school of his/her own, with or without a black belt, and with very little money. You can offset the odds of this ever happening by fairly compensating your top producers, helping them achieve their personal goals, and by establishing a solid relationship. This doesn't mean you should let employees with an over-inflated self-worth take advantage of you, but at times you many need to consider "sharing the wealth."

Clearly, it takes more than a weekly paycheck to keep the best employees long-term. If you want to prevent your top people from gracefully bowing out, then be careful not to get lazy when it comes to communication, compliments, recognition, support, leadership, compensation, friendship, rewards, patience, advancement, and overall relationship-building. In other words, don't take your best staff members for granted. As the excerpt below points out, eventually they might lose their enthusiasm, and leave.

Remember Me?

I'm the person who sat patiently for years while you refused to recognize my existence.

I'm the person who loyally gave you the majority of my waking hours, 50 weeks a year. And in return you took my self-respect and dignity. The only time you noticed my presence was when it was time to criticize.

I'm the person who after 50 weeks of tireless and above-average effort each year—effort I made because I believed in you and the company—got my review four weeks late, and received a raise exactly the same as the worst performer in my department.

Yes, you might say I'm the salt of the earth. A tower of strength. The kind of employee any company would be proud to employ.

But do you know what else I am?

I am the person who will never come back to work for you. By the way, it does amuse me to see you spending thousands of dollars every year to get me back, when you had me there in the first place. To think that all you had to do was listen to me once in a while, show me a little respect, a little appreciation. But you didn't. Anyway, I wish you all the luck in the world. (Excerpt from Keeping the Best, by Martin Yates)

46: Ten Ways to Appreciate Your Staff

Are you an owner, team leader, or manager of a martial arts school? If so, then it's important that you constantly remind your staff members how much you value all of their hard work, devotion, loyalty, effort, and accomplishments. Doing so will make them feel great, and motivate them towards peak performance. Here are 10 simple tips to help get you started.

1. Praise in Public

One of the most powerful ways to show a staff member that you appreciate them is to praise their efforts in front of others. This puts them in the spotlight, and encourages them to keep up the good work.

2. Give Compliments

What can make a staff member feel more appreciated than a genuine compliment from their respected leader? Okay, maybe two genuine compliments. You can never give enough, as long as you are sincere. When it comes to making staff members feel appreciated, giving regular and genuine compliments reigns supreme.

3. Keep Your Word

Dr. Stephen Covey says, "Trust is the highest form of human motivation." And one of the best ways to gain an employee's trust is to always be up front and honest with them. Never make false promises. Employees do not appreciate that, and will resent you for it.

4. Actively Listen

You can build tremendous rapport with a staff member simply by taking the time to patiently listen to them when they have something to say. Avoid pretend listening. Instead, listen with the intent to understand. They'll feel truly appreciated.

5. Recognize Accomplishments

It's tremendously gratifying to staff members when their leader recognizes their accomplishments. A congratulatory email, pat on the back, round of applause, award, or some kind words in front of their coworkers will go a long way towards making them feel appreciated. Not recognizing accomplishments can lead to frustration and disappointment.

6. Make Yourself Available

If you want to make an employee feel completely unappreciated, simply let them know that you are too busy when they try to communicate with you. The message this sends out is, "YOU ARE UNIMPORTANT." On the other hand, if you want your staff members to feel like executives, make time for them whenever they need your leadership.

7. Schedule Lunch

Taking a staff member out to lunch every now and again is one of the easiest ways to show them how much you appreciate them. Not only will it make them feel great, but it'll make you feel great as well… that is until they say, "I'll have the lobster!"

8. Create Incentives

Someone once said, "Nothing says thank you louder than a check." I'll let you be the judge of that one, but it's true that monetary rewards, year-end bonuses, performance-based incentives, or occasional gifts are great ways to remind staff members that you appreciate them. Often, gestures like these will encourage them to double their efforts for you.

9. Remember Birthdays

Okay, we've all suffered through too many off-key renditions of "Happy Birthday to You." But you gotta admit, once you get past the singing, birthday parties can make you feel pretty darn appreciated. That's why it's recommended that you not forget to celebrate your staff members' birthdays.

10. Host Gatherings

Inviting staff members to social gatherings is a great way to let them know you're thankful for all they do. Fun events that can be used for this purpose include Super Bowl Sunday, New Year's Eve, Fourth of July, holiday staff parties, etc. This is an easy way to build camaraderie, create team spirit, and show appreciation.

Of all your school's resources, its human resources are the most valuable. So never take your employees for granted. Instead, always remind them of how much you appreciate them. Do this, and your employees will work harder, feel better about their jobs, and smile whenever you enter the room.

47: Experience the Power of Networking

Networking is one of the most important things that you can ever do to grow yourself and your business. When you network, you acquire a whole new perspective. You meet new people, hear different ideas, and learn fresh approaches that you may have never thought of on your own. As a result, networking can speed up your growth, and trim years off your learning curve.

In fact, some of the most successful people I associate with are experts at networking. They are masters at the art of "brain-picking," and have learned to absorb others information like a sponge. Many top instructors I know constantly network with other instructors, to share ideas on curriculum, staff training, selling, demonstrations, testing procedures, marketing, organizing special events, etc. This gives them a major operational advantage over owners that don't take the time to network.

But there's one benefit of networking that is far more valuable than the rest. You see, networking gives you the chance to meet certain individuals who can help you achieve your goals much faster than you could on your own. If you're fortunate enough to team-up with such people, often they can open all the right doors for you. Indeed, this can expedite your growth by light years. At the risk of sounding cliché, it's sometimes not what you know, but whom you know.

Here are five ways that you can begin networking immediately:

1. Pick up the phone and contact one of NAPMA's NSSN Faculty Members. All of their contact information can be found at www.NAPMA.com.

2. Call NAPMA at our 800 number and ask one of our consultants to refer you to a NAPMA member school in your area.

3. As we discussed in section nineteen, one of the fastest ways to grow is to go visit a successful school and learn all that you can by watching how they operate. Be sure to call before your visit just to make sure the timing is okay.

4. Attend a large industry convention such as the NAPMA World Conference. This is one of the best networking opportunities you'll ever have.

5. Log onto a martial arts listserv or online idea-exchange forum, such as those offered on the NAPMA website.

Personally, I network all the time. I do it by phone, email, snail-mail, and in-person. Lately, as I've already mentioned, I've been networking quite a bit in person. In my opinion, that's the best kind of networking that you can do. Nothing can take the place of a successful in-person impression, or melding of the minds. Plus, when you meet someone face to face and they feel confident about you, they'll typically introduce you to all of their friends. Before long, you can build an army of contacts to network with.

In my experience, a school owner that doesn't network is like a bug under a rock. Often, they end up missing everything that exists outside of their own little world. This gives them narrow-minded perspectives relative to owners who network regularly. So make sure you keep up with your networking. It can really make a huge difference in your career... unless you're a bug!

Section Forty-Seven

48: Is it Time to Stop Making Your Landlord Rich?

In the last couple of years, I've noticed that a lot of school owners have stopped paying rent. Instead, they're buying their own buildings. Based upon my research, there are three main reasons why you may want to explore doing the same. These reasons include:

1. Wealth Building

This is the main benefit. At only $3,000 per month, you'll pay out over a million dollars in rent over the next 30 years. Why not invest that million dollars in a piece of property that you'll someday own? If you do, your property is almost certain to appreciate tremendously by the end of the term.

According to NSSN Faculty Member Dr. Harold Lauber, "I have 8,000 square feet and over one acre of land, which I purchased for $300,000. I pay a mortgage of $2,700 per month. We've had the property for 12 years, and I have been offered over a million dollars for it."

Likewise, NSSN Faculty Member Dale Cook tells me, "I own an 8,000 square foot facility, in prime retail space, in Tulsa, OK. I own this $600,000 property free and clear. Ahhh, what a feeling! Had I been renting, I'd still have monthly payments and zero equity."

These gentlemen are not alone. Many other martial arts professionals have stopped paying rent too. Now they're making themselves wealthy, instead of their landlords. Clearly, buying your own space could become your retirement income someday.

2. Income Generation

Some instructors I network with are buying their own building and then renting a portion of it out to tenants. This enables them to generate additional income that helps to pay down the mortgage over time.

NSSN Faculty Member Kristen Alexander has just applied this strategy. Mrs. Alexander comments, "We just built a strip mall for our third location. It's a 10,000 sq.ft. facility – 5,250 for my dojo, 5,250 rental space. The costs weren't much greater than if we built just our school and this way we generate rental income for ourselves! This is the right decision because I am in business for the long haul and it will continue to provide for my family even after I am just a memory!"

3. Tax Savings

When you buy your own building, there can be a variety of tax savings and incentives depending upon the owner's personal situation. The details surrounding this are way too complex and personalized to address here. However, according to my CPA, William Colasanti, "The pros typically outweigh the cons, as long as the overall arrangement is structured properly." When and if the time comes, my suggestion is that you seek some really good advice in this area so you do it right.

As you can see, there are some very good reasons to own your own school if such an endeavor fits your belief system and personal situation. It did for my good friend Brad Jones. He just purchased a building in Canada and transformed it into a gorgeous 8,000 sq.ft. temple-like dojo.

Brad's dojo used to be a movie theatre. In fact, he saw the movie Billy Jack there many years ago. Now he owns the place! Despite the stresses that went along with a massive renovation, Brad has doubled his square footage, while keeping his mortgage payment nearly equal to his prior rent payment. Plus, his commercial mortgage payment is locked in and won't increase as rent typically does. In 15 years Brad will own the building and you can bet it will appreciate considerably by then.

When asked to comment on this subject, Easy Pay President Rick Bell cautions, "When you buy your building you are then in the real estate business. You want to look at it from an investment standpoint. If you have to shut your school down for some reason, you'll still own the building." Rick raises a valid concern. You want to be able to service the note as fast as possible if things suddenly fall apart. The key is to make a sound property investment, because you may not be running a school out of your building in the future.

On a final note, I've had the opportunity to associate with a number of very wealthy people. These heavyweights all had one thing in common. They all owned lots of property. Heck, the value of my own home has more than doubled in the last six years. To that end, I encourage you to explore this avenue. Without a doubt, it's one of the best ways you can build wealth in the martial arts business.

49: Is Bigger Better?

Acommon question that crosses the minds of school owners around the world is whether or not to expand into multiple locations. Let's discuss some of the pros and cons concerning this very important executive decision.

First, let's look at some of the pros. Multiple locations can result in increased revenue from product sales, tuition, and special events. It can mean greater profit, clout, market dominance, exposure, and opportunity. In addition, having more than one school allows you to influence the lives of more people through quality martial arts instruction.

According to my colleague John Bussard, "Owning multiple locations has its benefits. Because I have three schools with approximately 1,150 students, we see tremendous momentum with referrals, word of mouth, etc. I'm able to offer a great benefit package to employees including health insurance, a 401k, and a good salary. This creates enhanced staff security and confidence. Also, being a multi-school owner gives me more freedom, since I have other people assisting with the operation of my schools. Last but certainly not least, it can mean a lot more cash for the owner."

Now, let's consider some of the cons. Opening a second school, for example, isn't always as easy as breaking a second board. It's often more like the difference between breaking one board and three or four boards, depending on your managerial skills. Your expenses, staff challenges, commuting time, liability, organizational demands, and overall level of stress may increase considerably.

According to NAPMA Squared developer, Stephen Oliver, "As a multiple-school operator, you must be a systems designer, people developer, and staff supervisor. I'm really not trying to be doom and gloom, just sharing with you that there is more to running multiple schools than being good at running a school."

As you can see, when you become a multiple location owner your role in the organization will change. You're likely to become less of a hands-on instructor, and more of a manager. You'll have to learn to get your work done through the help of other people. If that's not your forte, owning multiple locations may not be for you.

It's also important to point out that opening multiple locations can be very risky if you don't know what you're doing. In fact, many such ventures do not succeed because instructors expand prematurely. Telltale signs of this are:

1. Their first school has a weak active count.

2. Their first school does not have an abundance of staff.

3. Their first school is barely profitable.

4. They haven't yet learned how to manage their first school properly.

Owners that expand under these circumstances rarely survive. They seem to ignore the fact that the newly opened school has to rely on the resources of the original school until it can stand on its own two feet. Sometimes that takes longer than expected. When instructors can no longer fund or staff their second school they typically lose it. And if the first school was weak from the start, they may lose it, too. Unless you are careful, multiple schools will turn into multiple headaches.

There are three main elements that make multi-school operations work. Number one is staffing. You must surround yourself with great people, pay them well, and then delegate. Number two is a complete systemization of your operation. Your system must work well in your first school before you can apply it to other locations. Number three, you have to become a good manager, or hire a good manager, to keep the operation in check.

Finally, I'd like to point out that I've seen single location owners earn a better take-home salary, and live a higher quality life, than certain owners with several schools and a lot more students. Single school ownership can mean less stress, less overhead, a higher tuition, and a higher net income. On the other hand, I've met many multi-school owners that have profited handsomely. So, is bigger better? It can be. It just depends on what your goals are.

50: Give "the Little Guy" Some Respect!

The NAPMA membership base is as eclectic it gets. We have members with student counts ranging from 10 to 2,000. They teach arts spanning from Aikido to Taekwondo, Kung Fu to Judo, and Muay Thai to Tai Chi. Some of our members own 10,000 square foot monster schools, while others teach out of a vacant space at their church. You name it, and you'll find it amongst our base of member schools. It's a true melting pot of the martial arts.

One major reason for this is because NAPMA has always welcomed all professional martial artists regardless of their style, background, affiliation, or student count. At NAPMA, it doesn't matter if a member grosses a dollar or a million dollars. All members are treated equally, and with the utmost respect and courtesy. No one is left out, especially "the little guy."

So who is "the little guy" anyway? While there is no official definition, he is typically the school owner who has fewer than one hundred fifty students. He is often a part timer. He is the low profile instructor who doesn't appear on the cover of magazines, or up on the stage at conventions. He usually teaches martial arts, not for the money, but because he loves what he does. He wants to grow, but needs to find some direction. Basically, he represents the bulk of the industry, and the above is his general profile.

Unfortunately, we exist in an industry where a bigger-is-better mentality has been ingrained into the brains of nearly everyone for decades. ("Nearly" is the operative word.) This puts the "little guy" at a disadvantage. For example, the "little guy" does little for equipment companies with strict minimums on gear purchases. "The little guy" does little for billing companies that have a vested interest in how big a school grows. And the "little guy" does little for magazines seeking success stories. So the "little guy" usually gets little respect. He's just not "successful" enough.

In "the little guy's" defense, I want to make one thing very clear. Success is a relative term. After all, what is success in the martial arts school business anyway? Is it Tony Fournier with 700 students? Is it Mike Mertens with 1,700 students? Is it Tiger Schulman, who reports a twenty million dollar annual gross? I speak with school owners more and more these days who are generating seven figure annual gross incomes. Are these examples of success?

Or is success the story of someone like NAPMA member Steve Sturgeon who has 125 loyal, paying students? According to Steve, he's successful. Steve says he has a great life, a great wife, a great house, a great car, everything he wants, very little stress, and he even has plenty of time to go fishing on the weekends with his kids. Is that success? To many of the "little guys," it is indeed.

Again, success is a relative term. It's not for me to decide what constitutes success. That's up to you. What I will tell you is that, if you're struggling to make rent, if you're having difficulty providing for your family, if you can't afford to save for retirement, or you're just personally unhappy with your school's growth, then you are probably not "successful." You could probably use some help reaching your goals.

At NAPMA, we thoroughly enjoy working with "the little guys" for a number of reasons. First, we see their potential, and helping them grow gives us a chance to further impact the industry in a positive way. Second, our fee for service remains the same regardless of our clients' current size or future growth. Third, it's a whole lot easier to double the student count of an owner with 100 students, than an owner that already has 1,000.

At NAPMA, we have no reasons not to respect "the little guy," or any size school for that matter. As long as you have the desire to improve, you have our support!

51: Growing Amidst the Competition

Awhile back, my colleague Chris Natzke called the NAPMA office in a bit of a panic. He was worried because a new school was just about to break ground less than a mile down the road from him. Adding to his anxiety was the fact that his new competitor was a nationally-recognized chain school operator with a reputation for being a marketing wizard. Chris was deeply concerned that his business would soon take a hit.

Well, more than a year after Chris' competitor began teaching classes, we touched base on what had happened. The effects his competitor had on his school were clear. According to Chris, "My business has gone through the roof!" Chris reported that all his classes from Little Ninjas to Fitness Kickboxing were packed. His staff had never performed better. His product sales soared. His gross income broke previous monthly records. Despite the competition, Chris had raised his class tuition several times during that year, and he steadily invested in his retirement. Overall, his school had kicked some major butt.

As Chris' experience illustrates, competition doesn't always hurt you. In fact, it can be one of the healthiest things that can happen to your school. For starters, it can serve as a powerful wake up call that spurs you to work a little smarter, stay a little later, and sharpen your focus. Competition motivates you to eliminate complacency, laziness, and sloppiness. It inspires you to rally your troops, polish your skills, and truly get serious about running your school. It can help you grow.

Also, your competitor's advertising dollars will often increase the awareness of the very service you are selling. Instead of only you promoting the benefits of martial arts in your community, now your competitor is promoting them, too. All of this extra promotion typically reaches greater numbers of prospects, and thereby expands the entire market of potential new students.

A good example of how competition can increase market awareness occurs in the fast food industry. It's not uncommon to see a Burger King open up on the same street as a Mc Donald's. When this happens, do people stop eating at Mc Donald's? No. Instead, more people start eating at Burger King. Next, Taco Bell comes along, then a KFC, and so on. The more fast food restaurants that open up, the greater the public's awareness of fast food. Ultimately, more people begin eating it. While martial arts schools are drastically different than fast food restaurants, the same rationale applies.

Another benefit of competition is that it creates a quality barometer within the marketplace. It gives the market a gauge for measuring the quality of one service versus another. These days, people are comparative shoppers. This can be one of your strongest advantages if you're running one of the best schools in your area. But be careful, because the reverse also holds true. In my days as a Program Director, I would always support a prospect's decision to check out other local schools before making their final decision to join ours. In fact, I sometimes encouraged it. I knew that we offered the best service in town, and even though we were the most expensive, serious prospects almost always came back to enroll after shopping around.

Finally, while competition can be frustrating, it's just a reality of being in business. My advice is to not lose any sleep over it. After all, you have no control over someone opening a school down the street from you. It's better to focus on what you can control, such as how well you run your school. As Chris Natzke says, "I'm competing with six other schools, all within a two mile radius of mine, yet my school is rapidly growing. This just goes to prove that it's what you do that matters, not who's down the street."

52: What to Do When Your Competitor Joins the Same Professional Association

Few things in our field create more overreaction than when a school owner discovers that a local competitor has just joined the same professional organization, such as NAPMA. Often, this causes the school owner who was first-in to freak-out! In some cases, the school owner who joined first becomes so badly jaded by their own fears (False Expectations Appearing Real) that they actually dropout of the organization.

Leaving an organization, for this reason, is usually the worst of all possible decisions. Indeed, by quitting, you let go of any competitive advantage you may have had over the other school. That gives them full run of the show, and leaves you with nothing. To a competitor, this is a dream come true. What more could they ask for?

It's important to maintain your composure should a situation like this ever occur. You want to avoid overreacting, or making any hasty decisions. Instead, try looking at the big picture. You might just see that the situation is not as bad as it appears. The fact is that, besides your own pride, nothing else is likely to be effected by the other school having a membership with your organization. Frankly, it's not going to put you out of business, your students won't notice, and the public doesn't care.

So what's the big fuss all about? The most common concern of instructors in this position is, "Now, they have the same advertisements that I have." While this is true, it's also true that most schools don't advertise very much at all. Since print advertising is very costly, many instructors rely mainly on word of mouth or referrals, for generating new students. Other schools advertise strictly in the Yellow Pages. The point is that even though your competition is getting the same ads as you, there is no guarantee that they'll ever even use them.

Another thing to consider is that, if you're part of a school support organization like NAPMA, then you probably have access to a large supply of ads. If you've been with them long enough, you may even have a pile of ads that the "new guy on the block" has never even seen. So if you plan to advertise, just pick a different ad than what the other school is using. Furthermore, you can mix and match ads, advertise in different media than your competitor, or simply create your own ads from scratch. If you think about it, getting the same ads as your competition can be a pretty easy problem to fix.

In fact, external marketing is the only thing that's likely to "crimp your style" if a competitor joins the same professional organization. On average, ads are usually less than twenty-percent of what most companies provide. Everything else they do is aimed at improving the internal operations of the school. Despite this, most school owners who dropout of an organization, as a result of this issue, do it because of their erroneous advertising concerns.

Another common worry is, "They have the same marketing ideas that I have now." Yes, and they do kata at their school, too. Does that mean you should stop teaching forms? Again, most of the information that an association or support group provides is designed for internal use. That means it's up to each school's staff to implement the ideas before any of them can work.

The reality is that many instructors receive great ideas, but never follow-through on them. They simply file them away in their office, with all the other great ideas they never had the time or ambition to try. Also, most instructors only use certain aspects of a particular program. Others don't use any of it at all; they just want to belong. Knowing this, wouldn't it be a shame if a school owner dropped out of an organization that he could really benefit from, because of a new member who hardly even uses the materials?

On the other hand, many school owners have turned this potential negative into a positive. In other words, they've learned to work with their competitors instead of against them. For example, some owners combine their advertising dollars, and end up with larger ads featuring both schools. Others conduct seminars, network, run television commercials or host tournaments together. While cooperative arrangements such as these depend largely upon the circumstances surrounding each situation, many school owners have found a way to make them work.

So, if a competitor joins the same professional organization that you currently belong to, don't fly-off-the-handle. Instead, keep your focus, and simply continue doing the very best job possible at running your school. But, above all things, don't withdraw from the organization out of anger. Doing so would kind of be like cutting off your nose to spite your face.

53: Reacting to Challenges

A long time ago I learned that if you really want to see what a person is made of, watch how they react under pressure. That's when an individual's true colors will finally show. That's when you'll learn the most about their inner strength, integrity, and character.

Whether we're talking about our personal life, or our business life, the fact is that pressure-some challenges are always lurking. They're like weeds. You get rid of one, and another pops up. That's why it's so important that we learn to control our reactions to problems. If not, those problems may just get the best of you. The last thing your school needs is a leader with a nasty temper, massive stress, or a negative attitude. Over time, this will lead to problems with your business, and even worse, your health.

As a school owner you're constantly going to have little fires to put out, tough decisions to make, and problems to solve. There's always going to be a new headache, situation, or difficulty to deal with. That's the nature of being in business. Furthermore, that's life. You can't get out of it, so you've got to get into it. Read on!

You "get into it" by doing your best to control those factors you have some control over, such as your emotions, and your reactions to life's little challenges. When something goes wrong, you can choose to fly off the handle, get stressed out, feel sorry for yourself, take it out on others, punch a wall—whatever. (Yeah, feel that blood pressure skyrocket.) Or, you can choose to maintain your composure, stay positive, think it through, and calmly seek a solution. My suggestion is to be smart, but don't take life or yourself too seriously. That's the reaction I always do my best to choose when under pressure.

Also, I've found that it's best not to get all stressed out over that which you can't control. Why worry and get sick over something you can't do anything about? I'll be the first one to admit that this is much easier said than done. The key is to train yourself to subordinate emotions to what you know is the most intelligent reaction to the situation at hand. You've got to be strong, and fight hard not to overreact. This takes lots of practice, discipline, mental focus, and inner-strength. But you can do it. Again, while you may not have control over what problems occur, you do have control over the way you react to those problems. That's called having good self-control, and developing it is completely up to you.

Me? For a while there, I was letting all the little challenges that come with operating the world's largest professional martial arts association eat at me. Yes, it was causing me major stress. Yes, it was bringing me down. Yes, it was effecting my overall well-being because I was choosing to react negatively to the barrage of challenges I was continuously confronted with.

Then, I heard a quote that I'll never forget. A quote that changed my life. That quote, spoken by Dr. Stephen Covey said, "It's not what happens to us... it's our response to what happens to us that makes us what we are." The moment I heard it—ahhhhhhhhhhh—it seemed as though the heavens opened up. I realized that I had the power to choose my reactions to problems. The moment I applied this strategy I felt as though a weight had been lifted. My attitude, performance, and sanity all improved. At the same time, my stress level was dramatically reduced. I'll never go back to my old ways again. Eureka!

I believe that being able to apply Dr. Covey's advice autonomically is one big factor that separates a "student" from a "master," where self-control is concerned. I suggest you memorize his quote, internalize it, and keep it in your back pocket at all times. Take a deep breath, and recite it when necessary. I do this, and it helps me react more appropriately to the constant challenges I have to face.

54: "Criticism is the Price of Success"

Recently, I was communicating with a man who is considered one of the most successful and notorious CEOs in corporate American history. He's a man who has run numerous multi-billion dollar corporations, and in the process earned hundreds of millions of dollars for himself. In our most recent phone conversation, this no-nonsense corporate titan made a statement that really hit home. He said, "Rob, criticism is the price of success!" Without a doubt, I have found these words to be chillingly accurate.

It's been said that as one's success increases so does the size of the bull's-eye on their chest. When you're the underdog, scores of people come out of the woodwork to cheer you on. They slap you on the back, and chant "Go get 'em" or "You can do it!" They say, "We're behind you all the way." However, the minute you become successful, the cheers die down, and the criticism begins. As the lead dog, you can almost always count on catching plenty of thorns.

After years of consulting with school owners, I can tell you that a particular aspect of criticism frequently occurs in the martial arts. Here's a common example. One day, "Joe Karate" finally decides to get serious about running his school. Over time, "Joe" evolves from karate-jock to martial arts professional. He transforms his school from a dungeon to a modern martial arts academy. Today, instead of having 100 students, "Joe" has 400 students. He's earning a decent income, living in a nice neighborhood, driving a nice car, and he's somewhat high profile in his community.

Life is good for "Joe." However, not everyone is happy for his accomplishments. In fact, some of his karate buddies and competitors are so jealous of his success that they no longer associate with him. If "Joe" hosts a fundraiser or tournament, none of the local guys attend. Instead of supporting "Joe", they criticize him, and say things like, "Joe sold out," or "Joe's school is the Mc Donald's of karate." Because of his success, "Joe" has become persona non gratta, and one of the most criticized instructors in town.

My colleague Stephen Oliver comments, "The interesting thing in martial arts is that the schools around you that are not experiencing financial success always attack those that are successful with something to the effect of 'They're just a 'belt-factory'' or, 'Yeah, but they don't teach "real" martial arts.' This perspective continues, and is even believed by those who purvey it, in the face of evidence to the contrary."

The fact is that some instructors simply prefer to criticize their more successful counterparts, rather than get out of bed earlier, work harder, learn more, or innovate so they can achieve a similar level of success. Actually, doing this makes them feel important. So criticizing helps them compensate for their lack of accomplishment.

Where students are concerned, they typically criticize successful instructors from a different standpoint. As you grow, they begin to pay closer attention to everything involving you. They focus more on the things you say, what you wear, what you drive, and whom you associate with. You become a frequent topic of discussion. They put you under the microscope, and ultimately come to expect higher standards from everything you do. Of course, this often leads to criticism. But that's simply par for the course. Can you name any high profile leader or successful person who hasn't been criticized?

That having been said, my advice to you on criticism is simple. As long as you know in your heart that you're doing the right thing, let that criticism roll off your back like water rolls off the back of a duck. Never let it get you down, or break your spirit. Remember that your criticizers want to see you fail. That way, you'll be more like them. I suggest you think of criticism as rocket fuel for your career. Learn from it, and use it to launch yourself even higher. Do not let it catch you off guard. Instead, expect it. It's the price of success.

55: Beware the Plague of Politics

Before I started taking martial arts classes I played little league baseball for a couple of years. To this day, I'm still amazed at how much politics existed on that tiny field, hidden behind an Albertson's in St. Pete, Florida. The various team coaches hated one another, jealous parents were constantly at each other's throats, the umpires were crooked, and fistfights ensued on a regular basis. Thanks to petty politics, the league slowly wasted away, and our field is now an abandoned lot.

In many ways, the martial arts industry reminds me of my brief experience with little league baseball. We, too, are plagued with politics. Yes, politics. It exists at all levels, from schools and tournaments, to equipment suppliers and style associations. Politics is like a cancer that grows inside, eats away, and makes us weak. It's the main reason why our industry is so terribly fragmented. Politics is holding us back, retarding our growth, creating divisiveness, causing us to miss valuable opportunities, and forcing all martial artists to suffer its painful consequences.

Collectively, our industry must realize that in business one plus one equals three. Too often I encounter institutions that resemble fortresses, ruled by autocrats who strictly prohibit contact with the outside world. Their anti-synergistic actions only further the fragmentation that's holding us all back.

I, for one, have attempted to create unity among key organizations in our field, but have made little progress. Sometimes, alliances are blocked because self-serving men of relative influence pull strings from deep within the shadows. In other cases, the lack of cooperation stems from issues of control, ego, or power. I sum all these quagmires and others up with one word—politics!

As President for NAPMA, I have a powerful vision. My vision is to grow our industry by decreasing fragmentation and increasing unification at every level of participation. It's to maintain an open door policy with any quality organization that wants to work with NAPMA for the betterment of the martial arts. It's to elevate our industry into the mainstream along side of sports such as tennis, golf, soccer, football, and gymnastics. It's to destroy the plague of politics that infects us all. It's to affordably provide the highest quality educational resources so that instructors of every style can increase their professionalism, and grow their schools. And, it's to dramatically increase the number of students participating in quality martial arts programs worldwide.

That's my vision, and together we can make it a reality. But first, we must all set aside our differences, kick the politics, and be willing to do what's best for the good of the group. We're all in this together. I call upon you for your support.

56: Cut Loose the Chains

All professions are plagued with a small percentage of unscrupulous individuals that will take advantage of others, given the opportunity to do so. There have always been unlawful attorneys, hypocritical doctors, and thieving accountants. Unfortunately, the martial arts field has its fair share of criminals, too.

Sadly, this is not just my opinion. It is my direct experience, after having consulted with thousands of martial arts school owners throughout the years. In fact, you'd be surprised to know just how many times I've received phone calls from subservient school owners who call up to secretly consult about how they are being taken advantage of by their "Master," "Grandmaster," or "Association." Watching over their shoulder, and whispering into the phone, they describe some of the abuses they put up with.

Here are 11 of the most common complaints I hear.
1. Being forced to buy gis and equipment at full price from their "Pseudo-Master," instead of buying their merchandise wholesale from a gear company.

2. Having to turn over the majority of testing fees to the "Pseudo-Master," who is flown in for testing purposes only.

3. Having to pay a percentage of the school's gross income to the "Pseudo-Master," who does nothing to help out the school.

4. Paying exorbitant licensing fees to use the name of a school that is recognized by practically no one.

5. Being kept on hold for years longer than necessary before being tested for a higher belt.

6. Controlling what owners can advertise, or hang on the walls in their own schools. One NAPMA member claims that the "Pseudo-Master" came in, and ripped a poster off the wall, and tore it up, right in front of everyone. He didn't like the fact that the instructor and student in the poster were smiling.

7. Restricting the use of modern ideas that are proven to generate new students or boost retention.

8. Setting parameters as to what parts of town instructors can accept students from.

9. Forcing instructors to change the name of their school so as not to compete with the "Pseudo-Master," who just moved into town.

10. Belittling instructors, to make them believe they can't survive without the "Pseudo-Master."

11. Threatening to take away an instructor's rank, and blackball him/her from the association if they don't comply with the "Pseudo-Master's" rules and regulations.

This is just a sampling of how certain "superiors" in the martial arts field take advantage of naïve followers. You'd almost think these pseudo-extortionists were above the law, considering their Mafia-like approach to dealing with others. In my opinion, they are perpetuating a form of organized crime that's disguised by martial arts mysticism, and a self-created image of godliness.

Coincidentally, school owners who allow themselves to be subjected to these types of leaders typically have the smallest, least profitable, dinosaur-like schools in the area. According to the owners themselves, their school is the way it is because their "control-freak Pseudo-Master" has them in a straightjacket. They claim they are worked very hard, and make barely enough money to feed their families. Often, they wonder if they are school owners or indentured servants. After hearing them describe their situations, sometimes I wonder the same.

For example, many "under-the-thumb owners" are usually prohibited from implementing simple retention adjustments, like adding a stripe to a belt, which might actually keep students in the school longer. They are forced to make their students wait eight or ten years before testing them for black belt. They are not allowed to deviate from the archaic curriculum that makes the "Pseudo-Master's" system all that it is. The list of restrictions goes on and on. What a shame!

No one can take advantage of you without your permission. In today's society, there's absolutely no reason why an instructor should put up with this kind of abuse. First of all, there are plenty of excellent style-based associations out there that do not take advantage of their members in any way, shape, or form. They provide rank in a professional manner without subjecting their members to abuses like the 11 cited above.

Secondly, there's so much martial arts business information readily available from NAPMA and other organizations, that instructors no longer have to rely on a "Pseudo-Master" for any kind of business guidance whatsoever.

If you're an instructor who feels as though a certain superior is taking advantage of you, ask yourself these two questions. 1. What does my "Master" do for me that I can't do for myself? 2. If the "Master" no longer existed, would my school wither up and die, or would it begin to flourish?

I'll bet you can answer these questions without hesitation. I'll bet you're sick of being treated the way you are. Now, you just have to find the courage to cut loose the chains. Do it. You have my support!

57: The Perils of Dating Students

One of the most difficult issues a school owner can face is what to do when one of his instructors begins dating a student at the school. This is a very touchy situation that must be handled with extreme care. After all, both students and employees are involved, so the stakes are high. First, let's take a serious look at the liabilities this situation can create, and then I'll offer some suggestions that can prevent it from ever happening in the first place.

Clearly, school owners are subject to many potential liabilities when a staff member becomes personally involved with a student. But the owner is at his greatest risk when the couple starts to experience personal difficulties in their relationship. It is at this time that the school may notice some of the side effects of the quarrel.

In the midst of a dispute, the student may stop coming to class in order to avoid seeing their significant other. Conversely, an instructor is likely to become distracted if their "other half" shows up for class while the quarrel is still in progress. This could make it very difficult for an instructor to concentrate on teaching. That, in turn, could have a negative effect on the entire student body.

If the couple's argument is serious enough, the student will probably stay away from the school, indefinitely. Here, the owner suffers the loss of all tuition and other potential revenues the ex-student would have generated. As you know, this could add up to thousands of dollars. But the school could also lose a student's friends and family members, too, if a nasty break-up should occur. Depending on the circumstances, other students who are close friends or relatives will usually side with the ex-student, not the instructor. Soon, gossip starts, and everybody involved loses their focus for training amidst all of the social politics.

Even more, the owner risks losing his instructor if he decides to intervene. In fact, owners usually do end-up getting involved since they have a vested interest in the matter. But the emotional instructor may have a different view, resulting in a conflict of interest between the two. This can easily cause the instructor to quit or get fired, depending on the situation.

Ultimately, the school risks developing a bad reputation if a student-instructor relationship goes sour. This is especially likely to happen in smaller cities and towns, where word travels quickly. Nobody wants their wives or kids to train in a school where an instructor is known for "hitting-on" the students. That's not to mention what could happen if the ex-student was a minor. I'll leave that one up to your local newspaper to explain.

Indeed, there are a number of potential liabilities involved with student-instructor relationships. Now let's discuss what you can do to minimize your risks if you don't approve of this going on at your school.

1. Make a Decision
You must begin by taking a clear stand on this issue. Do you consider students at your school to be forbidden fruit, or not? Also, make sure that you set a good example yourself.

2. Create a Policy
Once you've decided how you feel about your instructors dating your students, type it out. Draw it up like a contract, and be specific as to your instructors' limitations, and the penalties they'll face for breaching the agreement.

3. Call a Meeting
When hiring new instructors or evaluating current employees, explain to them exactly how you feel about this issue. Do not beat around the bush. It's critical that you make yourself clear to avoid any future misunderstandings.

4. Present the Agreement
Request that your employees read and sign the agreement. This will ensure that they understand your position on this matter, and agree to abide by the rules.

5. Review Your Policy
This can be done in quarterly and annual review meetings with your staff. Simply ask each employee if they've had any personal interaction with your students. If the answer is "no", then move on to the next topic. But make sure they are reminded of this rule on a regular basis.

In conclusion, there is much supporting evidence suggesting that student-instructor relationships can be risky for school owners. However, there is also a flip side to this issue. Many instructors have settled down with, and are now married to someone who used to be one of their students. That includes both male and female instructors alike. Let's face it. Teachers spend so much time at the school, it's no wonder they may end up meeting someone there. So should student-instructor dating be prohibited, or not? That's for you to decide. In the end, I guess it just boils down to another one of those difficult to make executive decisions. I wish you the best of luck with it!

58: Hold Yourself to the Highest Standard

Leadership flows from the top down. That's why I always try my best to set the standard of excellence in all that I do. To me, this translates to many things. A few examples would be keeping in shape, staying positive, demonstrating the highest levels of integrity, working hard, constantly learning, never quitting, being kind to others, developing myself in every imaginable way, and so forth. Get the idea? In summary, I always make a strong effort to hold myself to the highest standard. I feel that this is my responsibility as a leader in both the NAPMA organization, and the martial arts industry.

Yes, I'll be the first to admit that making a constant effort to be your best is no easy chore. Frankly, it's very hard. Even knowing this, I still want to encourage you to do the same. Never settle for second best, let yourself go, or compromise your values. As a martial arts instructor, you are in a unique position. Kids think you're a super hero. Adults place you up on a pedestal. Your students look to you for leadership, guidance, and support. For these reasons and many others, I suggest you make every effort to set the standard for excellence in your world, just as I do in mine.

This brings me to the topic of self-discipline, a key component when it comes to holding yourself to the highest standard. So what is self-discipline, anyway? I've been taught that self-discipline is having the strength to do what has to be done, when it has to be done, whether I like it or not. Naturally, this is easy to talk about, and hard to actually do. But if you want to achieve your greatest potential, you'll have to employ this philosophy a whole lot more often than the average Joe does. Furthermore, you want to train your staff members to do the same. One of your goals as a manager should be to help your staff become more self-disciplined so they can achieve their maximum potential in life, as well. As a leader, always try to pull more out of your people, and incrementally raise the bar when you feel they're ready. Enhancing self-discipline is a great place to start.

On this note, I suggest you ask everyone in your next staff meeting to jot down his or her definition of self-discipline. Let them share their definitions out loud, and then give them the one you want them to commit to memory. Now here's some key points. Your staff will be a lot more self-disciplined when you (1) clearly teach them what self-discipline is (2) constantly help them develop their self-discipline in a positive manner and (3) prove to them that you yourself are actually self-disciplined. Do this, and you'll see tremendous results both personally and professionally.

According to NAPMA's NSSN Faculty Director Charlie Foxman, "To me, holding myself to the highest standard means truly living the martial arts way, and walking the walk. How can you preach it if you don't do it?"

I agree with Mr. Foxman. You've got to practice what you preach. If you want your staff to work harder, then you work harder. If you want your students to train harder, then you train harder. Your responsibility as a leader is to lead by example, and inspire others to raise their standards to your level in virtually every way. Likewise, never lower your standards for others who try to pull you down to their level. This includes everything from losing your temper with a difficult parent, to doing something that's flat-out dishonest. As a business owner, you will be tempted every now and again. Do not give in. Always stay in control, and keep your integrity high.

Finally, please realize that your school will only be as good as you. Over time, your school will actually become a mirror image of you. That's why it's so critical that you maintain a sterling image, continue to grow, and let your performance take you to the top. In other words, always hold yourself to the highest standard.

59: Fourteen Ways to Improve the Martial Arts Industry

After 19 years of martial arts training, and nearly 10 years at the forefront of the martial arts industry, I've paid my fair share of tuition to the school of experience. I've learned that there are many things our industry could do to improve. While this passage may not provide you with detailed solutions, I do promise that it will spark your creative imagination.

Imagine the impact on our industry if, collectively, we could:

1. Sharpen the sales skills of anyone selling martial arts memberships. Imagine the millions of extra students who would be actively training in our industry if only our professionals were better skilled at sales. Attending seminars and reading up on the subject of sales is a good first step towards achieving this.

2. Get more schools to offer a greater diversity of services. E.g. Little Ninjas, Fitness Kickboxing, Judo, UBC, etc., These types of additional programs will attract more people to our schools, and better fund our core martial arts programs.

3. Inspire more of the industry's professionals to embrace self-education through NAPMA membership. Since there are no educational prerequisites for employment in our field, it only makes sense for owners and their staff to self-educate.

4. Raise tuition rates for all new students entering our schools, while safely grandfathering the current students in at their current tuition rate. Unfortunately, many schools still undervalue their service. (According to a variety of sources, the national average for tuition is about $100 per month.)

5. Rethink the "bigger is better" mentality when it comes to operating a school. Bigger is not always better. Quality of student, and quality of life is more important to some.

6. Decrease fragmentation and increase unity. Petty infighting and politics only hold us back. That applies not only to martial arts schools and competitors, but also to industry organizations. Don't hold grudges, or be reluctant to bury the hatchet.

7. Improve phone skills. The phone skills in many schools need some serious polishing. The good news is that this is easy to fix, especially with NAPMA's Way of the Phone program. With a little practice, you'll see huge improvements fast.

8. Teach more structured Leadership Team programs that offer true value for participants. To help with this, NAPMA has created the Guidance on Leadership Development (GOLD) program. This excellent curriculum details the A-Z on operating a comprehensive Leadership Team program.

9. Increase basic business knowledge. Many school owners are admittedly "black belt" martial artists and "white belt" business people. However, ongoing self-education through NAPMA membership can go a long way towards improving business skills.

10. Conduct less freak show martial arts demonstrations. I know *Ripley's Believe It Or Not* enjoys the material, but it ruins our image, and creates stereotypes.

11. Become more comfortable with delegation, especially in the area of marketing. Many school owners still have "black belt eyes." In other words, they advertise what appeals to them, and not necessarily what appeals to the public. More widespread professional marketing, such as the kind that NAPMA inexpensively provides, would further enhance our industry's image, and our collective student count.

12. Implement more modern curriculums and teaching methodologies, as suggested by the American Council on Martial Arts (ACMA). This would dramatically improve the interaction between students and instructors, and lead to higher retention in our industry.

13. Invest in more professional-looking facilities, with better equipment, and higher standards on maintenance. How, you ask? See point number four to the left.

14. Hire more Program Directors to share the workload, especially in the area of critical administrative procedures. I've found that it's very difficult to operate a successful commercial school without a top quality Program Director. If you don't have one, begin looking for one today.

60: Are We Destroying the Image of Black Belt?

Recently, while on an airplane, the passenger sitting next to me noticed me thumbing through the newest issue of Martial Arts Professional (MAPro). He was a big fan of the martial arts, but had never trained. To satisfy my own curiosity, I asked why?

My co-passenger explained that a friend of his was a so-called "black belt." He had seen his friend practice, and was convinced that the guy couldn't fight his way out of a wet paper bag. He went on to detail how his friend practically had his black belt handed to him on a silver platter because of his rich dad's money and influence in the community. The guy also mentioned that some of the young children in his own family were black belts. According to him, these kids were still in grade school, and didn't even take their martial arts training seriously. So he felt that there simply wasn't anything special about being a black belt. His perception was that it was a waste of time and money.

In some ways, I can understand why my fellow traveler felt the way he did. It seems as though anybody can earn a black belt in certain schools these days. The standards for achieving rank seem to be diminishing. Recently, this was made clear to me after visiting several tournaments and studios. Many of the adults and kids running around with black belts, in my opinion, simply had no business wearing one. These "black belts" couldn't hit a proper balance, they didn't blade their feet, their fighting skills were poor, and you could easily see that their skills have never been tested under fire. An ordinary punk off the street would probably eat 'em alive in a self-defense situation. Sometimes I look at students like this and wonder, "Is this a black belt?"

The answer to that question is not for any one person to decide. There are too many variables involved. However, my instincts tell me that the way some instructors are preparing students for black belt could really use some improvement. This is especially obvious when it comes to children's instruction. Many of today's instructors have de-emphasized their standards for proper technique and skill, and overemphasized weak character development curriculums. Some instructors have even tried to force-feed such material to the adults.

It's important that we stay focused on the development of actual martial arts skills, such as proper form, effective sparring, and competency in self-defense. In my opinion, a child or adult that can't display proficiency (for their age) in these fundamental areas should not be awarded a black belt. We need to raise our standards, and not make it too easy for students to earn their black belt. Otherwise, we're sending a message that says, "Earning a black belt is a waste of time and money."

Relatively speaking, the quality standards in many martial arts schools were much higher a decade or two ago than they are today. In fact, these standards were usually too high, and often unrealistic. So the percentage of students who earned a black belt was a fraction of what it is today. But the students who actually went on to become black belts were usually highly competent technicians, and extremely serious about their training (and slightly dysfunctional, too).

Even when I began my training in the mid-eighties, making black belt was very difficult, and highly prestigious. All aspects of the training were geared towards perfection. Those of us who eventually made black belt were the ones who were too stubborn to quit. We didn't mind getting our ribs crunched, or our eyes blackened. We were the ones that never missed a class, and then enjoyed beating each other's brains out on Sunday mornings when the school was closed. We put up with the negative reinforcement, the belittling comments, and the frequent injuries. After many years, this regime transformed us into dangerous fighters and exceptionally talented martial artists. Earning the rank of black belt came with heavy price, but it really meant something.

I'm lucky to have seen both ends of the spectrum when it comes to black belt training. What I've learned is that neither the "new school" nor the "old school" way of creating black belts is perfect. They both have their flaws. I mean it's not good to have such low standards that we just give away black belts to anyone and everyone who pays tuition at our schools. This just waters down the arts, and destroys the image of black belt, as my co-passenger on the plane perceived. On the other hand, we can't be so tough with our students that only one-percent of them make it to black belt. It's difficult to pay the rent when all you have is 40 or 50 cold-blooded killers training at your school.

The solution, I believe, is to find a happy medium. This means creating an effective curriculum, providing quality instruction, and keeping your standards high. It's the best service you can provide to your students, and it's the only way we'll keep from destroying the image of black belt.

61: "The Roots Under the Tree"

Recently, I was walking through an outdoor mall after conducting a business seminar. I was stunned when I saw a small child walk towards me wearing a T-shirt with F.C.U.K. boldly written across his chest. My eyes suddenly widened in amazement. What stunned me even more was that his father was walking behind him wearing a larger version of the same F.C.U.K. brand T-shirt, and mom was pushing a baby stroller with an F.C.U.K. hat on her head. I could hardly believe what I was seeing. It made me sick!

My brief encounter with the "F.C.U.K. Family" reminded me just how much society needs the positive, traditional aspects of martial arts training. If these folks were martial arts students, I bet they would have been a whole lot more conscious of their image. I know that I was, as a student, and I still am today because of my training. In the old days, my instructor would have put me on my knuckles, in the parking lot, if he caught me dressed like that in public! My instructor taught me respect, courtesy, and discipline. My training gave me self-worth, esteem, confidence, and leadership skills. For these reasons and more, I would have instantly subordinated that shirt to my values as a martial artist.

In case you are not aware, tradition is critically important to me—kata, bowing, the gi, respect, courtesy, discipline, humility, spirit, integrity, etc. These elements make us martial artists. In fact, tradition is what separates martial arts instructors from P.E. teachers. It's the traditional qualities of our training that make our students so much more than fitness kickboxers, jocks, or common street fighters. Furthermore, I believe that the amazing results our industry consistently generates is largely due to the core traditional values and philosophies that echo through our classes. That's why I passionately encourage you not to loose sight of tradition as time marches on. As new generations of instructors emerge, we must be careful not to become a faded Xerox, of a Xerox, of a Xerox, where tradition is concerned. Tradition helps us to change our students' lives for the better, and positively impact our society. Let's never forget that.

However, there is a caveat. Tradition by itself can hinder growth. It can result in small student counts, financial distress, and in some cases it has even put schools out of business. Over the years, I've consulted with thousands of school owners, and I can tell you from experience that I've seen many instructors struggle because they are too traditional, and opposed to any kind of change. They end up holding themselves back, and they cause their students to quit. The secret to success, in my opinion, is tradition with innovation. Tradition without innovation, or innovation without tradition, can leave an instructor incomplete. I highly recommend a balance between the two.

On this note, I recently had an in-depth conversation about tradition with my colleague Joon P. Choi. He is brilliant when it comes to this particular subject matter. In our discussion, Master Choi pointed out that he is a very traditional martial artist, and he runs his school using traditional philosophies. Tradition is his foundation. But he is also an innovator. He has brought modern teaching methodologies into his school, new programs, and many additional profit centers. He is forward-thinking, and a sharp businessman. In fact, he is a martial arts millionaire, and living proof that tradition with innovation is key.

I'm proud to say that over the years NAPMA has paved the way for many traditional martial artists to modernize their teachings in a manner that does not compromise the integrity of their art. We have helped countless instructors incorporate alternate profit centers into their schools, and to dramatically improve the quality of their lives. We will continue to do this for our industry, going forward because we recognize the value of tradition with innovation. As Master Choi said, "Tradition is like the roots under the tree." At NAPMA, our mission is to nourish these roots, but to also make sure that the flowers on the tree have what they need to blossom.

END

Notes

Notes

Notes

Notes

Notes

For Walter,
mentor and friend

Martha Speaks copyright © 1992 by Susan Meddaugh
Martha Calling copyright © 1994 by Susan Meddaugh
Martha Blah Blah copyright © 1996 by Susan Meddaugh
Martha Walks the Dog copyright © 1998 by Susan Meddaugh, originally published as
     a Walter Lorraine Book
Martha and Skits copyright © 2000 by Susan Meddaugh, originally published as a
     Walter Lorraine Book
Perfectly Martha copyright © 2004 by Susan Meddaugh, originally published as a
     Walter Lorraine Book

www.hmhbooks.com

ISBN 978-0-547-57967-2

The text of this book is set in Excelsior.
Book design by Rachel Newborn

Printed in China
LEO 10 9 8 7 6 5 4 3 2
4500324766

MARTHA SPEAKS

STORY TIME COLLECTION

by Susan Meddaugh

HOUGHTON MIFFLIN HARCOURT

Boston   New York

CONTENTS

HELP!
THERE'S A DOG IN MY HEAD!

The stories in this collection exist because my seven-year-old son asked a marvelous question about our dog. The dog happened to be Martha, and the question was "If Martha dog ate alphabet soup, would she speak?"

A perfect question from a young mind that hadn't yet ruled out a world of wonderful possibilities. I knew he was kidding, but an instant image popped into my head: Martha's brain filled with alphabet soup letters. And who better to experience this life-changing event than our Martha.

Martha was a stray, a mutt, a combo plate of breeds. A friend, who had briefly taken her in, said she looked like a Dalmatian/beagle cross. We took her home, and our vet added pit bull to the mix. Whatever her genetic DNA or life before we adopted her, she had a personality made from many interesting parts. She often seemed subtly human in the way she viewed the world. But she was undeniably friendly and expressive.

photo by Ruth Gray

Her body language spoke very clearly. She was independent, a free spirit. Off leash in the meadow, she raced out to greet people, dogs, and horses. She chased squirrels and chipmunks, and eventually joined us after our walk, back at the car.

By the time Martha was six years old, we had added another dog to the family: Skits. But Martha was always the alpha dog, and Skits always deferred to her. She was the queen.

I loved drawing Martha, and she had already appeared in earlier books, sometimes simply as a portrait on a wall. When I pictured her pasta-filled brain in my head, it wasn't hard to believe that if Martha could talk, given her personality, she would have a lot to say. Lots of opinions, but also a lot to learn. As it turned out, after the success of *Martha Speaks,* she had more books in which to explore her gift of gab. I think she would say that she did her best in her books to help people become more knowledgeable about their "best friends."

photo by Ruth Gray

I continue to hear her speak inside my head. And speak. And speak. And speak.

—Susan Meddaugh

For the Finneys

The day Helen gave Martha dog her alphabet soup,

something unusual happened.

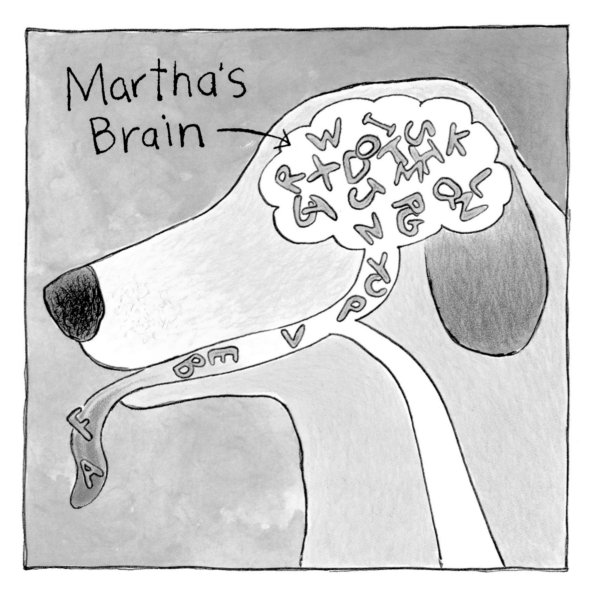

The letters in the soup went up to Martha's brain instead of down to her stomach.

That evening, Martha spoke.

Martha's family had many questions to ask her.
Of course, she had a lot to tell them!

Alphabet soup became a regular part of Martha's diet, and the family had a wonderful time surprising people. Walking the dog was always good for a laugh.

They ordered pizza from a different restaurant every night.

They taught Martha how to use the phone.

But this was a mistake.

Pretty soon, more than pizza was being delivered!

Family and friends were amazed.

Although there were those who doubted,

Martha always had the last word.

But there was a problem:
now that Martha could talk, there was no stopping her.
She said exactly what was on her mind.

She made embarrassing comments.

And, she always told the truth.

Occasionally she wondered why
her family was often mad at her.

15

But she kept on talking.
She talked through everyone's favorite TV shows,

except her own.

She talked while they were trying to read.

There's a poodle over on Circuit Street I'd really like to play with. He's small but what a dog! And speaking of small, I'm sure you're all curious about the early days of my life...

She talked and talked . . .

I was born in a back alley to a poor but loving mother. Although she was a mixed breed, Momma was determined to raise us puppies right, to give us a solid background before we went out into the world at eight weeks. Even before our eyes were open, Momma would say: "You're dogs! Not cats! Don't ever forget that!" Blah Blah Blah Blah Blah Blah Blah

I still remember the rules Momma gave us to live by: ① Beware of Two-year-old humans with clothes-pins. ② Under the table is the very best place to be during a meal. ③ Never mistake your human's leg for a tree.

...Blah...
Blah Blah...
Blah Blah... Blah (that was for my brothers, of course.) And...
Blah ④ if it's black and white and smells funny,
Blah Blah   Blah   it's not a cat. Don't chase it.
Blah Blah Blah.   And while we're on
    Blah Blah   the subject, I
        understand Cat, but
        I can't speak it.   Blah Bla
    Wait... where was I?   Blah
        Oh yes.... Blah
    Blah Blah Bla

18

and talked . . .

until her family could not stand it and said, "Martha, *please!*"

"What's wrong?" asked Martha.
"You talk too much!" yelled Father.
"You never stop!" yelled Mother.
"Sometimes," said Helen,
"I wish you had never learned to talk."

Martha was crushed.

The next day, Martha did not speak. She didn't ask for her dinner, or to go out. She offered no opinions, but lay quietly beneath the kitchen table.

At first her family enjoyed the silence, but after a while they became worried.

"What's the matter, Martha?" asked Helen.

Martha didn't answer.

Helen's father called the vet.

"There's something wrong with my dog!" he said.

"She won't say a word."

"Is this some kind of a joke?" snapped the vet.

Helen offered Martha bowl after bowl of alphabet soup,
but Martha had lost her appetite for letters.

Martha's family wondered if she would ever speak again.

Then one evening when her family was out, Martha heard the sound of glass breaking.

"A burglar!" she gasped. "I better call the police."

She carefully dialed 911.

But when she opened her mouth to speak—

Martha hadn't eaten a bowl of alphabet soup in days!

Martha raced to the kitchen.
She barked. She growled.
She tried to look ferocious.

GRRRRRRRR

The burglar wasn't frightened. He picked up a pot from the stove.

"Uh, oh," thought Martha. "It's taps for sure."
But to her surprise, the burglar put the pot down
on the floor in front of her.
"Here, doggy," he said. "Have something nice to eat."

The burglar smiled as he closed Martha into the kitchen
and went back to work.

"Dumb dog," he said.
"Lucky for me you like alphabet soup."

When Martha's family returned, they found the police
removing the burglar from their house.
"How did you know he was robbing our house?" asked Helen.
"We got a call at the station," said the officer.
"Some lady named Martha."

"Good dog, Martha!" exclaimed her happy family.
"You're so right," said Martha.

Now Martha eats a bowl of alphabet soup every day.
She's learning what to say and when to say it, and
sometimes she doesn't say anything at all . . .
at least for a few minutes.

For Niko, Harry, Sandy, and *Poppa*

Martha was always a talented dog.

But when she ate alphabet soup, something truly surprising happened. The letters went up to her brain instead of down to her stomach . . .

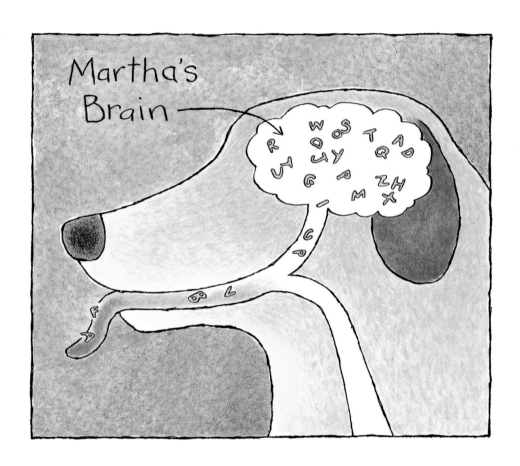

and Martha spoke.

Martha loved letters. She lapped up consonants, and savored every tender vowel.

Martha loved words. Lots of them. Separately, or strung together in endless sentences.

But there were three words Martha hated.

These words meant she was never welcome in restaurants . . .

or in any of her favorite stores.

And people were so rude.

This was confusing to Martha because when she called
the same places on the telephone, people were always polite.
On the telephone they never said: "Hey! Are you a dog?
I'm hanging up if you're a dog!"

Martha loved the telephone. She could talk for hours.

One day she entered a contest.

Martha won a free weekend for four at the cozy Come-On-Inn.
Her family was thrilled.
But when the official notice came in the mail,
there was a problem.

"I have an idea," said Helen. She and Martha disappeared into the attic. When they emerged:

Martha's family packed plenty of alphabet soup and set off for a wonderful weekend at the Come-On-Inn.

A small crowd had gathered to welcome them, and Helen
introduced her grandma, *Martha.*
"Congratulations, Martha!" said the manager of the inn.
"These flowers are for you."

But Martha was not interested
in flowers.

Martha's family rushed her past the other guests and up the hill to their room.

"Let's go for a swim," said Father.

"Then we can have a game of Ping-Pong," said Helen.

"And a nice picnic lunch," added Mother.

"Sounds like fun," said Martha.

But Mother said, "Sorry, Martha."

"I'll sneak you out after dark," said Helen.

"Sit and stay," said Father.
"Hmmmph!" thought Martha. "Same old story."

Confined to the room, Martha was depressed . . . until her eyes fell upon an old friend.

Her belly full, Martha fell into a deep sleep.
She didn't hear a soft knock on the door. She didn't wake up
when the chambermaid came in to leave fresh towels.
Then the chambermaid saw the bones,

the empty wheelchair,

and Martha.

She ran screaming from the room.

That woke Martha up. She wandered down the hall to find out what was going on.

"Of course I'm mad," Martha said.

Everyone stopped and stared in absolute disbelief.

I won this contest, fair and square. Me. Martha. And I'm not having any fun at all. Why? Because I'm a dog. D. O. G. Dog. A smart dog. But... there are NO DOGS ALLOWED in this hotel. Everywhere I go — No Dogs Allowed! The Butcher Shop... the Supermarket... No Dogs Allowed! I CAN'T BELIEVE IT! Dogs have been by your side since you were in caves. Ten thousand years of loyalty, and we still can't go into a restaurant and order a steak.

A lifetime of canine companionship and what do we get? A week in the K-word while you go off on a "family" vacation. Am I missing something here? Aren't we part of the family? We're your Best Friends! Or did you forget?

"Why is everybody leaving?" asked Mother when the family returned from their swim.
"Uh-oh," said Helen. She spotted Martha . . . sitting with the manager.

But the manager was smiling.
"I wonder if Grandma, I mean Martha, would be
interested in summer employment?"

The next day, the cozy Come-On-Inn got a new name, and Martha started her summer job. Pets are now welcome at the Sit-n-Stay Hotel, where the soup du jour is always alphabet, and the hostess is never at a loss for words.

Business is grrreat!

For three Js, one D, and Cisco

Martha was always a great communicator.

Sad ↑

Happy ↑

Mad ↑

But when she ate alphabet soup, the letters went up to her brain instead of down to her stomach,

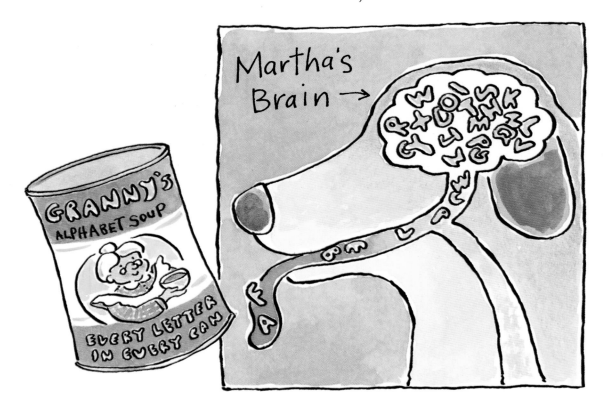

and Martha spoke words.

Martha loved letters. She loved words.

So Martha's family gave her a bowl of alphabet soup every day.
Martha never missed a meal.

Having words opened up a world of possibilities for Martha. All the employees at the local Burger Boy knew her well . . .

and the neighborhood dogs depended on her.

Of course, Martha couldn't help but notice how much her family enjoyed having a talking dog. How special they thought she was.

There was someone else who loved letters as much as Martha. Alf Abbott was the A man at Granny's Soup Company. He made all the A's that went into alphabet soup.

Alf loved his job, and he was good at it. He assumed he would always have it.

Unfortunately, the new owner of Granny's Soup Company, Granny Flo, had other ideas. Granny Flo was looking at a portrait of the founder, Granny Elsie, when she made an important business decision.

But she was really thinking, "Fewer letters mean bigger profits."
So Granny Flo summoned her twenty-six alphabeticians and
began to draw letters from a hat. Thirteen
alphabeticians were
suddenly out of work.
One of them was Alf.

Within a week, cartons of the new soup
went out to local supermarkets.
"No one will even know the difference,"
thought Granny Flo.

But several days later, after finishing
her daily bowl of alphabet soup,
Martha said,

"What did you say?" asked Helen.

Helen giggled.
"How embarrassing!"
thought Martha. "Must be a touch of laryngitis."

* Good soup today.   **I said: Good soup!

But it wasn't laryngitis. Strange sounds continued to come from Martha's mouth all day.

* Something is wrong.   **My words are gone.   ***Woof.

The next day wasn't any better.

*Hello. Gus has a short message.
**I'd like ten burgers. BURGERS! BURGERS!

Martha ate bowl after bowl of alphabet soup, but it was no use. Nothing she said made any sense at all.

"I'm afraid Martha is losing her ability to speak," said Helen's mother.

*No good.

"Oh, no!" thought Martha. She couldn't imagine not being able to talk. No more Burger Boy? No more telephone calls? Just another dog, scratching the door to go out.

And what would her family think if Martha lost her letters?

"I couldn't stand that," thought Martha, and she went outside. She walked down the street, away from home, mumbling to herself.

*My words are gone.   **Where did they go?   ***What to do?

Martha had wandered for several hours when a familiar aroma reminded her that she had missed something important.

She followed her nose . . .

*Soup's on!

and her nose led her directly to Alf Abbott's kitchen, where
Alf was heating up a can of soup.
"Come in," said Alf, who missed his friends from the soup
company. He poured Martha a big bowl of alphabet soup.

Martha ate her soup happily, but without expectations, while Alf just gazed at the bowl in his lap.
"There it is!" he said. "A perfect A. And look at that L. Boy, Lou sure had a way with pasta."

Alf continued to admire each letter in his soup until Martha was almost asleep, lulled by the sweet sound of vowels and consonants. Then Alf said in the saddest voice, "My last can of *real* alphabet soup. It's just not the same since Granny left out half the letters."

The words came out of Martha's mouth perfectly clearly.

Martha didn't know whether to laugh or growl. To Alf's absolute astonishment, she started to sing.

Then she said,

Martha found Granny Flo in her office.

She got right to the point.

Granny Flo turned angrily in her chair,
but all she could see was Granny Elsie, looking right at her.
Granny Flo was terrified!
"Did you speak?" she asked the portrait in a small voice.

"Every letter in every can," said Martha from behind the desk. "You promised!"
"But it was good for business," said Granny Flo to the portrait.
"Good *soup* is your business," said Martha.

Granny Flo made the first of thirteen calls from beneath her desk. She began with A, of course.

Martha was feeling better in every way when suddenly she heard familiar voices calling her name. Then her whole family was hugging her and talking at the same time. They were saying wonderful things . . .

and all before Martha could even say a word.

MARTHA WALKS THE DOG

For Martha

Martha's family had a wonderful party trick.
They knew that when they said:

Martha would.

Guests were always amazed.

Martha learned to speak the day she ate alphabet soup. The letters went up to her brain instead of down to her stomach.

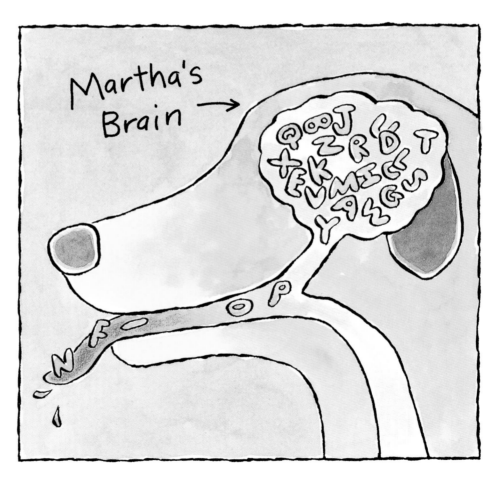

Martha's Brain →

Martha's family was so proud.

But Martha never let flattery
go to her head.

Martha loved her daily walks.
As usual her pals were scratching,
sniffing, or snoozing, and Cisco
was chasing Nelson the cat.

But there was one difference. A house down the street had
been sold, the FOR SALE sign replaced by a new sign.

Martha went to investigate.

She was puzzled. She didn't see a dog.

Suddenly a mountain of fur burst from under the porch stairs, lunging and growling at Martha.

Before she could say a word,
a man came out of the house.

BAD DOG, BOB!
BAD DOG!!

Bad Dog Bob retreated to chew
on his chain.

As the weeks passed, Martha hoped that Bob would calm down. But every time Bob saw Martha he charged to the end of his chain and barked ferociously at her.

 It wasn't just Martha. Bob barked at anything that moved.

WOOF WOOF WOOF

His owner was just as ferocious.
On Martha's daily neighborhood rounds
she always tried to ignore their angry
barking and yelling.

BAD DOG, BOB! BAD DOG!

One day on her walk Martha
heard a nicer voice.

"Thank you," she said.
"What's your name?"
"Thank you," said the parrot.
"What's your name?"
"My name is Martha," said Martha.
"My name is Martha," said the
parrot.
"Hmmm," thought Martha.

Then Martha had an idea.

Martha had to stop the lesson when two people came into the room.

"Words are such fun," thought Martha.
She turned around just in time to see Cisco chase Nelson the cat into Bob's yard.

In a flash Nelson was through the yard and over the fence.

Cisco was a manly poodle, but he was no match for Bob.
Martha spoke up immediately.

She unleashed a torrent of words as Cisco made his escape.

Bob walked slowly toward her, but Martha wasn't worried.
She knew he would soon reach the end of his chain.
But when Bob came to the end of his yard he kept on walking.

I NEVER thought I'd say this, but... you are a BAD DOG! I think I speak for the neighborhood

"Can we talk?" asked Martha.
Bob opened his mouth . . .

WO

OF!!

and Martha ran for her life.

Round and round Bob chased Martha.

Nothing she yelled had any
effect on him.

Martha was running out of words and breath.

Finally she could run no more.
She closed her eyes and prepared to die.

And then she heard a voice from above.

GOOD DOG!

Martha opened her eyes.

She couldn't believe
what she saw.

BOB WAS SMILING.

"Great dog!" said Martha.
"Great dog!" said the parrot.
Bob's hackles went down.

Bob's tail began to wag.

Just then Bob's owner came running up.
Martha sank back into the bushes.

"Don't yell," Martha whispered.

"Don't yell," said the parrot.

"Be nice," Martha whispered.

"Be nice," said the parrot.

"It's a miracle!" said Bob's owner.

"Good dog, Bob," he said. He didn't yell.

"Looks like the beginning of a beautiful friendship," thought Martha. And she continued to walk the dog.

For Linda and John

Martha's family had a little surprise for her.

Within days of Skits's arrival, the house was in chaos.

Martha enjoyed the show from the safety of her chair.
She remembered being a puppy.

But one day Skits did something unforgivable.

Martha decided it was time to take charge.
"There are only two rules around here," she told Skits.

135

She explained how the letters
in the soup went up to her brain
instead of down to her stomach.

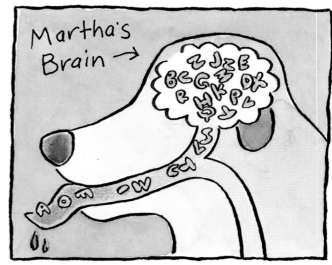

"Someday you'll be old enough for your own bowl of alphabet soup," Martha told him. But Skits wasn't listening.

At first Skits was an equal opportunity chaser and chewer, but he soon began to specialize. *Anything airborne.* He couldn't resist a flying object. Outside . . .

or inside

"GRRRRow up," said Martha.

Before long, Skits did.

But nothing really changed.
Skits continued to chase anything flying
through the air.
He just couldn't help it.

One morning Skits found his family gathered in the kitchen.
"It's time," they announced.
Instead of one bowl of alphabet soup and one bowl of kibble,
there were two bowls of alphabet soup on the kitchen floor.

Everyone watched as Skits ate his bowl of soup. They leaned closer, eager to hear his first words.

"That's it!" they said. "More soup."
The family made sure that every letter in the alphabet was there in the bowl. Again they waited as Skits finished his second helping of alphabet soup.

This time he said:

ARF!

Martha wondered about Skits's brain. Was it too small? Maybe there wasn't room for twenty-six letters.

"Oh well," Father said. "I guess two talking dogs was too much to expect."

Skits wandered out into the yard and lay down. He knew his family was disappointed in him. Martha was special. He was not.

His gloomy thoughts didn't last for long.

ARF!

Skits always enjoyed a good bug chase.
But this was his first taste of yellow jacket.

"YEEOWWOWWOWOW!" he howled when he bit down on the angry insect. The pain was terrible. Skits tried to run away from it. He ran and ran, but the sting stayed right with him.

Many miles later Skits came to a stream and gulped down the cold water. At last his mouth felt better.
The he looked around and realized something. He was lost.

When Skits didn't come home, the whole family set out to look for him. They walked down every street and talked to everyone they met, but they didn't find Skits.

That night, while her family made signs, Martha stayed by the phone. "I'm sure he's okay," she thought. "Maybe someone has found him."

On the other side of town, Skits spent the longest, loneliest night of his life.

"If only I could talk," he thought.

The next morning the family gathered their signs and began the search all over again.

Everything reminded them of Skits.

"Skits would love this," said Helen sadly, pointing to a sign on the tree.

"That's where he'll be!" shouted Martha. "All those flying objects in one place all afternoon!"

"You're right!" said Helen. *"He can't help it."*

Martha and her family watched and waited through every event
at the Frisbee competition. Multicolored disks sailed through the air
for hours, yet there was no sign of Skits.

The final contest of the day was the Chase for the Golden Frisbee.
As the yellow disk sailed across a blue sky, every dog in the park,
including Martha, took off after it.

Then from the opposite end of the park came a flash of familiar fur.

It was a dog so fast and focused on the flying disk that all the other dogs stopped in their tracks. All the other dogs except Martha.

A cheer went up from the crowd.

"What a catch!" they shouted. "That dog wins the Golden Frisbee!"

On the way home Helen said, "Martha. You missed the Frisbee. You never missed before."

Martha just smiled.

That night Martha and Skits each ate a bowl of alphabet soup.
Skits opened his mouth, then closed it. He still couldn't speak.
"That's OK," Martha told him. "You are a specialist in flying objects."

For Marguerite
and
for Vicki,
the voice of Martha

"What did you say?" asked Mother.

"I mean, soup, please," said Martha.
Mother smiled and fixed breakfast for Martha and Skits.
The two dogs began every day with tasty bowls of alphabet soup.
As usual, the soup went straight to Skits's stomach.

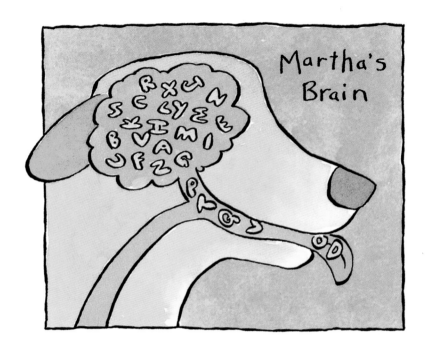

But the letters in Martha's soup went to her brain.
And Martha spoke.

After breakfast, Martha and Skits strolled downtown.
On Main Street they joined a crowd of people.
"Friends," said a man in a green suit, "what do dogs want?"
Before Martha could answer, the man continued.
"They want to scatter trash on pickup day, sleep on the furniture, and drink from the toilet. They drool and bark and scratch their fleas. And they would always rather chase a squirrel than come when you call."

Then the man said:
"Is that what people want?
Your dog may be your best friend,
but he could be better. I, Otis
Weaselgraft, will show you how.
Sir Lancelot," he called. "Come."
A sturdy pug approached the
dog trainer.

"Sit!" said Otis Weaselgraft.

"Get down!" he said.

"Roll over!"

"Beg!"

"Hop on one paw!"

After this impressive demonstration, Otis Weaselgraft said: "Sign up today for my THREE-STEP TRAINING PROGRAM. Tomorrow you'll have a *perfect pup,* just like Sir Lancelot."

"Hmmmph!" Martha said to Skits.

Word of the new dog trainer and his amazing program traveled from neighbor to neighbor. Soon half the dogs in town were enrolled at the Perfect Pup Institute.

At the Perfect Pup Institute, Martha and Skits slipped in to observe the latest graduating class. They watched as every dog obeyed every command.

They sat.

They got down.

They rolled over.

They begged.

They hopped on one paw.

Finally Otis Weaselgraft placed a dog biscuit in front of each graduate.
"Wait," he said, and every dog waited.

Skits couldn't believe his eyes.
With a hungry "Woof!" he bounded forward and gobbled up
every single biscuit.

Otis Weaselgraft was not upset. It was a perfect opportunity
to show off his program. He placed another biscuit
in front of each dog.
"Good dogs may now eat their biscuits," he said. "Chew slowly.
And, please, no crumbs and no drool."
Four perfect dogs did exactly as they were told.

Outside, Martha consulted with Skits.

Martha didn't see Otis Weaselgraft's quiet partner, Dr. Pablum.
"A talking dog!" he gasped. "I've got to find out how she does that."

The next morning Martha began an investigation of the Perfect Pup Institute. She was wondering how to get inside when Dr. Pablum swung open the door.
"Come right in!" he said to Martha.

Dr. Pablum escorted Martha to his laboratory. But before she had a chance to look around, he pushed her into a crate and locked it. "Speak!" said Dr. Pablum. "I know you can."
Martha did not hesitate.

"I knew it!" said Dr. Pablum. "Weaselgraft!" he shouted.
"A talking dog! I'll be famous!"

Otis Weaselgraft came into the lab. He looked at Martha.

"You're working too hard," Otis Weaselgraft growled at Dr. Pablum.
"Get rid of this mutt. She's not even a paying customer."
But Dr. Pablum had big plans for Martha.

Otis Weaselgraft stomped out of the room. He soon returned with a dog who looked like Sir Lancelot. But this dog wasn't acting like Sir Lancelot.

"Fix him!" Otis Weaselgraft snapped at Dr. Pablum. "We can't have this happening during a demonstration."

Dr. Pablum put Sir Lancelot into a crate next to Martha and left with the pug's collar.

"Sir Lancelot," said Martha.

"Burt," said the pug, in Dog. "They call me Sir Lancelot, but my real name is Burt."

He slumped in his cage.

"I used to run with the big dogs," he said mournfully. "But look at me now. A demo-dog. No better than a robot."

Before Burt could answer, Dr. Pablum returned with his collar. He slipped it onto the struggling pug.

When Dr. Pablum left again, Martha called to Burt.

But this time Burt didn't respond. He just looked straight ahead.

It's the collar! thought Martha.
She watched as Otis Weaselgraft and Dr. Pablum embarked on their Three-Step Perfect Pup Program.

Step one:
They removed the dogs' collars.

Step two:

They attached a tiny object to the inside of each collar.

Step three:

They put the collars back on.

Now every dog was staring straight ahead. No tails wagged, and no fleas were scratched.

"Come," said Dr. Pablum, and all the dogs followed him to the front room.

Otis Weaselgraft opened the crate and pushed Martha out the back door of the Perfect Pup Institute.

When Dr. Pablum returned to his lab he was horrified to discover the empty crate.

"Really, Pablum," said Otis Weaselgraft. "There's no such thing as a talking dog."
Dr. Pablum was *furious*.

He raced to the back door to look for Martha.

"I'll tell you MY One-Step Talking Dog Secret," Martha said,
"if you do one thing for me."
She whispered in his ear.

"Yes," said Dr. Pablum, who was still very angry,
"I'll do it."

In the front room the owners had gathered to see their pets perform.

"Otis," Dr. Pablum said, "your collar is a little crooked." He reached up and made a small adjustment.

"There," he said, giving the back of the collar a pat.

"Now *you're* perfect."

Then, from someone hidden in the shadows, came a command.

Four dogs sat. And so did Otis Weaselgraft.

"Get down!" said the voice.

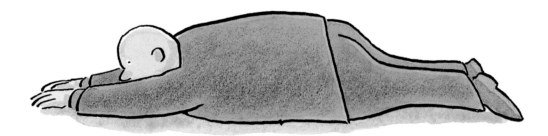

"Roll over!" she said.

"Beg!"

"Hop on one paw . . . I mean foot!"

Finally Martha said, "Speak. Tell the truth about the
Perfect Pup Program."
Otis Weaselgraft began to talk.

I'm not really a dog trainer. We put a microchip
in your dog's collar. The ROBOROVER Brain Blocker.
Shuts off every part of the brain except the
OBEDIENCE lobe. Turns dogs into furry robots.
Lasts about a month... just long enough to take
your money and move to the next state. Tried
it on cats last year. The Purrfect Pussy Cat
Program. What a CATastrophe! Cats don't
even have obedience
lobes.

ARF

ARF

ARF

ARF

While the angry owners were removing the collars
from their pets, Dr. Pablum cornered Martha.
"Quick," he said, "what's the secret?"
And Martha, who never broke a promise, told him.

"Very funny," said Dr. Pablum. "Now tell me the real secret."
But, seeing the owners approaching, he beat a hasty retreat.
Dr. Pablum was still puzzling over what Martha meant by
"soup" as he boarded the bus out of town.

Things are back to normal in Martha's neighborhood. Most of the Double PPs had to admit that having a perfect pup was really no fun. Something very important was missing. So once again dogs scatter the trash and drink from the toilet. They bark and scratch their fleas and sleep on the furniture.

But they also greet their owners with wagging tails and slobbery kisses.

Isn't that what people really want?

WOOF!

ARF!